BOOK OF SECRETS

ART OF THE CAR SALE

GARY L. SWANSON

Other books by the author:

Car Sharks and Closers
Close It Or Lose It
Hire-Education For Job Seekers

CONTENTS

INTRODUCTION

This is the most complete auto sales negotiating manual ever written. It contains the most successful sales closing techniques ever perfected!

You will find complete negotiating strategies along with the exact details that allow them to work every time. No word tracks to memorize; only the methods that make every negotiation a success!

Learn the dramatically refined techniques of effectively negotiating car sales at maximum profits and 100% customer satisfaction on every sale!

You will find individual chapters on every important subject; from your dress attire to grooming tips and proper ways to "meet and greet" (critical to your success), to your exact procedures to bring the buyer to the bargaining table.

Every single technique and method included has each earned hundreds of thousands of dollars in my commissions over a career of 18,000 sales, and I perfected them to work far better than anything else!

This teaching will be highly compatible with your dealer training and it will not conflict in any way.

Make your car sales career more fun and get paid doing it! How about a 20 percent raise!

Thank you,

Gary L Swanson

FOR THE NEW OR PPROSPECTIVE SALESPERSON

Welcome: Coming into the car business can be an intimidating experience. As in any new endeavor, you have a lot to learn and it's often coming at you from many different directions at once. Don't let it worry you one bit! The mere fact that you chose our profession and had the fortitude to get the job is what counts.

The next great decision you made was to buy this book. Now you've got it made. Your success is guaranteed!

In my early career, I was influenced by the story of the great Carthaginian general, Hannibal Barca. When Hannibal set out to destroy Rome, history says that he had anchored his ships and landed his powerful army containing vast stores of arms, elephants, and all essentials for defeating the massive Roman army. As they embarked toward the Alps that they would first cross in their venture, a cry of alarm echoed through the ranks. His ships were burning! To ensure their success, Hannibal had left orders that they be burned. The message he thus conveyed to his followers was that retreat was no longer an option. They had only one choice and that was to win!

Since you have joined the greatest sales profession in the world, you need to "burn your ships." You cannot afford to consider failure as an option. No other career will be as rewarding as this one, so accept the fact that you've chosen well and study this book; and never be afraid to attempt different methods. The customer will never know if you make a mistake, so you are your only critic.

If you have purchased this book as an aide to prepare for an interview to get a sales position, I'll mention a few things that may make it easier to land a job. When hiring new salespeople, I'd ask why they wanted to sell cars. I always cringed when I'd get answers like, "I love cars," or "I love people." These answers do not impress me. The person I'm looking for is the one who answers with, "I want to make lots of money!" I honestly don't give a hoot about cars. If you want to spend your time around cars, go hire on in the service department.

Pick the dealership you want to work at. Don't think you have to start out in a small store until you learn the ropes. Simply pick your store, and go in and get hired. All the credentials you need are this book. When you've read it, you're ready!

I am reminded of a friend who responded once to a dealer's request for his resume with this; "I normally just attach a copy of the yellow pages and circle the dealership I'm working at." When you're that good at selling, you really can afford to be a bit cocky; that dealer was being a pain!

GREETING

Let's talk about the varying ways about how we get face to face with a customer.

There are many ways by which salespeople receive their customers: some are on a rotating system; some are required to *call* the customer, so the first salesperson to spot the customer calls out "up," as in up to bat; yet others may be working at an *open floor* operation where whoever gets face to face with them first is the winner. Whatever method used, the first step in any sale is to *be there*.

The first example I'll use is; the salesperson is on the lot when a customer drives in, so you may politely ignore them until they park, and if nobody beats you to the people, you may have an *up*, so take control by making eye contact through the windshield and help them park.

This is your first opportunity to help, but be careful. Never have a customer make a *right hand* turn into a parking space. If the customer must turn down a right hand aisle, find a parking space on their left. When they have parked, and before your greeting, it's a nice courtesy to say something like, "Great job! I couldn't have made it in that spot as easily as you did."

Now, you and the driver will have your first contact; do not immediately stretch out your hand like a bellhop reaching for a tip. Relax with a, "Welcome to XYZ Ford, what brings you in to see us today?" The customer likely came in for a purpose and not looking for a new friend; so until you ascertain their reason for being on your lot, you have not earned the right to an introduction.

If they say they wish to use the restroom, don't risk a refusal to shake your hand, just don't offer. Now you can lead the folks to the restrooms, and at this point, you'll likely ascertain what they are interested in afterward, because it's highly unlikely that the restroom was their goal when they drove in.

When they return, ask if they washed their hands. *Just kidding*, to show you how you can relax with people once you take the self-imposed seriousness out of the equation!

As we know, there are many varying methods of getting before a customer. Another method previously mentioned is a rotating "up system" whereby the customers are taken in order from a list of salespeople on duty. They will rotate the order of their names on a list begun upon the start of their shift. No picking or choosing on this one, simply the luck of the draw.

There is still another method by which it is first come, first served. I've worked at a lot of these houses, but it's really embarrassing when 10 salespeople are running after a vehicle as the customers look for a parking place. This method definitely rewards the most aggressive salespeople, who also make the most money in most of these "pressure stores," and you really have to apologize to the customers you just won, but you only have to say, "See how valuable your car is to us; hope you're trading it in!" Now the episode is forgotten and you have the customer, and they will appreciate the bit of humor after being chased by the *mob!*

This is a business that rewards the hardest efforts. Fortunately, every auto dealer operates differently and you can pick and choose which one to work for.

Another method of selecting a customer is by the salesforce being sequestered in a separate bullpen or staging (observation) area. Some have large rooms directly behind the showroom, separated by massive one way glass. Many, with large salesforces, have bleachers in these rooms whereby all salespeople have a view of the dealership entrances.

When a customer drives in, the first person to "call" the vehicle, such as, "Up on the 4Runner," gets the opportunity. In this manner, only one person greets the customer and they never realize there is a whole room full of "backup!" This is the most professional, because no knife-fights will happen! Long ago, but not recently.

This leads to our next subject which is one of my pet peeves!

CELLPHONES

In a lot of auto dealerships, you can look around and half the salesforce is talking on phones; often times more than that!

No; please do not even think about defending these distracting critters; and no, they do not help you do your job!

Let's analyze this "money robbing" convenience that kills sales. I have always made it a rule that cell phones stay in a salesperson's desk or pocket and remain off. They leave a voice message that they, "can't come to the phone, but to please leave a message and that they will return all calls between certain times;" such as 10 to 11 in the morning and 2:30 until 4:00 in the afternoon. In this manner, no important calls are lost, and your silly friends who have nothing to do but talk, can still bend your ear when you return their call. Yes, you can check periodically and return calls as you please, but try to avoid socializing!

Give your most important family, like your spouse and parents, your work number and tell them to have you paged if it is an emergency. Otherwise, you're here to work, not chit-chat. No, you would not love working for me, however you would make so much money you could afford to hire someone to spend hours every day talking with your friends. You could give them a good salary and still make a great living. Cell phones are the greatest convenience, and a salesperson's biggest enemy!

NEGOTIATING STRATEGIES BY BOTH SIDES

There are many ways to begin negotiations and they only vary slightly. Let's look at the method whereby the salesperson constructs an offer with the customer having answered the buying question by saying they will buy the vehicle and drive it home right now. They prepare a trade-in appraisal slip and when they go to the sales office to pick up their scratch paper, the desk manager gives them a hit figure (starting price to offer) for the value of the trade vehicle. Then, the negotiating begins, but *we always commit first.*

If you are new to our business, I will quickly explain; if we sit there and ask the customer what he's willing to pay for ours and what he wants for his, and then we write it as an offer, we then put ourselves in a position of having to take away from what he thinks is a reasonable offer. Why does he believe his offer is reasonable? Because we wrote it down without challenging it. Anytime you write down a customer's offer, he believes that in your mind you must believe it is a possibility, otherwise you would object. Remember, the customer believes that you are in the know and this is all a game on our parts. This is why we always suggest what we believe the numbers should be, and these numbers are given to us by the sales desk; however, we tell the customer that they come from our memory. Our suggestion is based on our knowledge and experience, and therefore we believe that our numbers are what it will take. In this manner, we are opening negotiations by making an educated guess rather than an outright offer. Then, when the customer makes his counter it will be a lot more reasonable and although we respond by expressing doubt that his offer has a chance, we will try our best for him. This is the absolute rule; we always start first.

Because of the fear of the negotiating process, some people are often apt to respond to a dealer who advertises a "kinder and gentler" way of buying a vehicle. The theme of these programs of course is to appeal to the customer's fears. I have had hundreds of people that have asked me this almost exact question; "Why can't you people be honest enough to give us your best price and a fair value for our trade-in so we can answer yes or no?" My answer to them is always the same, "Because you wouldn't buy it." This question is usually asked by ladies, and it's always the same exact words. So is my answer, because they stop short; and then I explain that the reason they wouldn't buy it is because then how could they be certain that my offer was fair. So they would go from dealer to dealer and it would never end. Once I explain it, with the husband generally nodding in agreement (almost always), I put my hands on their shoulders and say, "trust me, I'm a car salesman. I'll treat you fair." With this delivery, I smile broadly, and now I have acknowledged their fears, and we are now on the same song sheet; so we all trust that I will be honest to a degree. They will sometimes roar with laughter and some sort of a loud outburst. You know what? All the pressure was released and the laughter is infectious. We have become friends and they do trust me.

Please believe me when I say that you must be relaxed, and I do not care if there are 20 people in the place all negotiating quietly and somberly with their salespeople like they're studying funeral plans. This is a fun business and when you can get your customers having fun, they will be as spontaneous as you are and they lose all of the intimidation that these other people I mentioned are laboring with.

I like to also tell the people the truth. "Bob, Mary; if I sold you this car for the sticker price, the manufacturer has cut our profit margin to the bare minimums, so you absolutely cannot pay too much." Then, depending upon the people, I add, "So I'm going to have to steal your trade." Yes, I have done this a lot, but I caution you to go carefully into this level until you have a lot of experience under your belt. My purpose in explaining my personal methods is not to by any means suggest that this job is not to be taken seriously, but to show you that it is not like one might expect; so enjoy yourself.

The reason customers fear the process is out of self-preservation. They know that salespeople are going to be friendly, but they also know that they are going to be told that this dealership is run differently. This owner insists that his people never lie, or most of them are seminary students, and a line of bull a mile long. There are so many phony bunkum stories out there that it's no wonder people are afraid. Why bother to try selling people on how your dealership is so honest and give them the pitch everyone else does? You know, and they know, it's a line anyway.

So here I come with off the wall comments like, "Trust me, I'm a car salesman" and "You'd better watch your wallet," and responses to their tough questions like, "Do I have to tell the truth?" and when they answer, "Yes, you do," (they always will) and I answer with, "You're asking a lot from a car salesman," then we laugh a little more and the trust is growing. I'm throwing this in because salespeople often take themselves entirely too seriously. Lighten up. Who do you think makes the most money in the circus? Is it the bareback riders or the clowns? Speaking of the clowns; I was doing my act once and leased a car to the circus master for the Ringling Bros. And Barnum & Bailey Circus and we had so much fun; two days later the paymaster came in and leased an identical car. No; they already had enough clowns! Thanks for asking.

Let's look now at the situation where your store has a closer or manager that closes all sales or in a circumstance where you need the assistance of a manger because you cannot close the sale and are at an impasse and need help. Whenever you are introducing a new face into the equation, you must forewarn your customer and you need to explain that you are doing so for your customer's benefit. Period. You will never win by running in a new negotiator. Any new face coming in is naturally presumed by your customer to be there only to help pressure them into submission; to get more money from them. They will view this new arrival as their enemy. Therefore, you must set the stage by carefully explaining to your customer that their business is important to you and since you want to do the best job for them that you can, you are going to need some help. You can say, "John, June, when my boss hired me, he hold me that if I ever need his help to ask; so, with your permission, I'm going to ask him to join us. His name is Jesse James and he's a great guy." Isn't that better than some slob who shows up and plants his fat ass in the chair and says, "Hi, I'm Bubba."

Now you leave to get your manager, and with the proper set up, your buyer's will be looking forward to the manager coming in. Whenever I came in, my salespeople had me set up as some sort of miracle worker, so the customers were glad to see me. Now if you're doing this introduction of your manager, there is what I consider to be a mandatory rule. There is no second choice. The salesperson must remain with the customer from here on out. If you are doing it any other way, you are doing it wrong. Your manager is there to help, not take over!

The professional line-close operation can only be done with the salesperson never leaving the customer's side after the closer has been introduced into the equation. This is a team effort for the customer's benefit and you'd better not deviate or you make yourselves out to be liars, and the manager is immediately presumed to be just another negotiator. Work this correctly and you will succeed beyond your wildest imagination, but do it wrong, and you are like every other car hustler in town. Can you tell that I mean it? I should mention that a lot of stores make the first salesperson go out and get another up, but again I will reiterate; never play that game! If you are to make high gross and great CSI, the original salesperson stays.

Another point to remember when you are negotiating is cut out the old bullshit scenario where you work under the premise of; "It's us against the house." That's old school and it insults the buyer's intelligence. Everyone, including the big boss (desk manager) and the owner all have the same goal; to earn the customer's business. When I tell you these things with such passion, it is because I am a master closer and an absolute authority on the art of the car deal. Trust me, I'm a car salesman. Even if they would be dumb enough to believe you, it sets a bad precedent.

So what happens when they know our game plan? We roll with it. Due to the preponderance of line-close systems in cities where I have worked, and quite often when my salesperson introduced me, they would speak up and say something like, "Hey let's not kid each other, I know the whole game you people play." I would step back, put my hands up and loudly reply, "Then you know that I is da closer." We'd all laugh, and I'd sit down and do everything I always do.

You can see that I can only stand to be serious for so long, and then like the buyer, I have to ease the pressure. Let's now look at some more strategies.

When you are in the midst of negotiating and a buyer makes a counter offer, be cautious that you do not be too quick to write it down. Remember that car buyers believe that our process is largely a game. They are suspicious that the salesperson and managers they are negotiating with are acting. When we are running around trying to make their deal and the salesperson is stumbling in their newness, the buyer feels this is all a well-rehearsed act. See, the customer even believes if we blow our lines, it's only an act. Makes it easy, right?

Because of this perception, when the buyer makes a counter offer, we must be careful in responding. Take your time, repeat the offer aloud, and *ask how they arrived at their figures*. Do not immediately write down their offer; because, in the customers' minds, they feel that you know where you're at in the deal. Therefore, if you quickly write down their counter, they feel that you believe that management will accept their terms. Buyers give us more credit than we deserve. Take the time to discuss their offer in comparison to the figures you were given by the desk and always defend your manager's offer. Always convince yourself that it can't get any better than where you are at. If you can sincerely show that you are certain that this last offer is as good as it gets, your demeanor will convince your customer. By showing genuine concern over earning their business, you can end negotiations earlier and make higher profits.

If you are in a position where you, as a manager, are closing the sale and you are also doing double-duty as your own desk manager as I have had to do so many times, it's even harder to stay strong. You know exactly where you are in the deal, so you have to be super strong. Often when I am sitting there with a straight face telling the buyer my boss is getting upset with me because I'm not getting to a point where he can break even, and in reality, I'm sitting on a four thousand dollar profit, it sure brings on the perspiration. I go into the sales office, make a slight change in the computer screen, grab my big, black permanent marker and in big, bold print, make my counter offer. Then as I leave the sales office and as the door closes, I say, "Thanks boss, I appreciate it." Then, with a wide grin, I excitedly rush back to present the new offer to my buyers. That's when you hope some dummy doesn't stick his head in the same door and ask, "Where's the boss?"

Yes, if you're wondering, I have quite often had buyers who wanted to personally thank my sales manager for making them the great deal. Each time, I had to explain how my manager had asked me to thank them so much for their business, but he had to rush home for "some special reason" and couldn't wait until they were through with the paperwork. Was this wrong to do? Were the customers happy? Great; that's all that matters.

Now, back to the negotiating of this deal; we must be able to look them in the eye and be absolutely convincing that we're all in; there is no more room. Period. Then, shut up and keep looking them in the eyes until you win. That's power. Don't worry about the customers getting up to leave; we have their keys in the sales office and if they do get up, your desk manager will be there to meet them and put everything back together again. Once the deal was done and the buyers are happy, I have had many, many people ask is there is actually anyone in the sales office. That's when I'd bring the boss out to meet them, unless he had left.

You must realize that the public is not stupid. They play the game sometimes better than we do. To prove my point that they play games too, is that I never had any trouble getting them to sit back down again if they bounced to their feet! Sometimes customers like to jump up, blow off steam to ease their tension, and then they're fine. Never overreact to their antics; stay calm, because they may be acting.

Early in my car career, I was fortunate to have worked in a few dealerships whose policies were to push every customer to the max, for all the profit we could get. I say fortunate, because it gave me knowledge about human behavior that I never could have learned in more conservative stores. I learned early on that the buyers play more games than many dealers could even imagine.

One of their strategies is to act mad and jump up and walk out the door toward their car. They know you won't let them leave.

I've been told by customers that they read that the proper way to buy cars is to go through this act in order to quickly get to their best deal. So for you dealers, managers, and salespeople who are worried about being kinder and gentler; I say, "Fuhgeddaboudit." The customer is way ahead of you. This is part of what makes our business so great. We get well paid for acting and the buyers also get rewarded for their parts as well. After all, you can't get too angry over a game; can you?

CREATING THE INITIAL OFFER WITH UNCOMMITTED BUYERS

After we have done the trade-in walk around with the customers and they are seated with refreshments, the salesperson excuses him or herself to get some scratch paper. Now I'll show you my method for a successful write-up. I created this over the years, and it has made it so much easier. In this scenario, we do not start by taking the customer statement (credit app); as we would if we had a normal buying situation. Reason being, is that this customer has not agreed to, "Buy and drive it home now." They have come in only to see what the "figures look like on paper."

Ask yourself this; why would any buyer in his right mind wish to give you all of his personal information and sign the paper which would allow his credit report to be run? They'll fight you on it and for this reason; you're swimming upstream. If they give you permission to run credit first, before you earn the right, their credit is quite likely bad anyway.

Therefore, always get right to the deal. This is why the customer followed you inside. You invited them to "step inside and see what the figures look like on paper," right? Then that's what they expect. This is where the magic comes from. When we come inside, we should usher our customers to a desk, table, or wherever we plan to create magic. Then we show them where the restrooms are and take their refreshments order.

Okay, so once we do this we go into the sales office for our scratch paper, right? Now, I will hand my appraisal sheet on the trade-in to the desk manager and while he or she is entering the information, I pick up a customer statement (credit app) and a work sheet on which I will work my deal. I fold both papers in half and place the worksheet on top, plain sides out. Why; because when I come back to the table I want my scratch paper to look like *scratch paper*! Now I will get my starting figure for the trade-in. We commonly refer to it as a "hit figure," because we (of the old school) say "Hit 'em with six grand." That is how we open negotiations from out of the gate, and without a computer created and printed form. If your store uses a printed computer generated proposal form, you can use it the same way and present it first. It will have the hit (starting figure) on it, and you just present it first while the customer statement remains folded.

I will place my scratch paper casually to my left (I'm right handed) and as I'm sitting down, and while maintaining eye contact with my buyers, I casually peel off the top sheet (work sheet). The buyers will not even pay attention to the other piece of paper (customer statement), because as I sat down, I opened the dialogue and we were all looking at each other. You may ask, "Why all the elaborate planning?" Because I've done this thousands and thousands of times and I now have it down to a science. And it works better this exact way. Thanks for asking. For further explanation; the customers are only expecting to come in and have a cup of coffee and have you show them the "figures on paper," as you promised. Therefore, if you sit down with an open worksheet with its needing to be filled in and a detailed credit application (they're not stupid), they are going to react with either an oral objection or at the least, a negative mental image of what you're going to put them through. Any cooperation after that is dubious.

In this example, if I don't have a preprinted offer form, I open my worksheet and it only calls for their names, address, and phone number which they readily provide. Now I write down the full list price which I took from the window of the vehicle they drove before we came inside, so they know what it was because I had them "check it" with me to make sure I got it right. Make certain to always do this with the buyer; it saves any questions that could arise and if you miss this step, they may frequently question the price. I also had them participate further by reading the VIN to me. Now I write this price in the proper place on my worksheet. As you say it aloud, you write the price down. You say, "Johnny, June; the price of the (car, truck, etc.) you're buying is thirty-eight five." If your price is $38,500.00, you *don't* say thirty-eight thousand five hundred dollars. The proper pronouncement is, "Thirty-eight five." Make the price sound *small*. Never draw it out if you can shorten the impact. By the way, did you catch the "price of the car you're buying" statement? Yeah, it was subtle huh?

Conversely, like a trade-in that's worth $19,500.00, you never say your trade in value is "nineteen five;" you say your trade value is "nineteen thousand five hundred dollars." See how that sounds so much larger? On *Wheel of Fortune*, you'll note that Pat Sajak will always say, "You won nine thousand three hundred and fifty dollars." Never does he say $9,350.00. Remember, shorten the impact of the selling price, and lengthen the trade impact. Like *Wheel of Fortune*, when Pat draws out the number the contestant won.

When you write the price in the space provided, you always preface it by addressing your customers by name. We want to have their undivided attention, and saying their names gently fixes their attention on what you are about to say. If there is a problem or misunderstanding of the price, it will now come up. Any objection such as, "We aren't paying that for it" will surface here. If there is no trade-in, we can rest on this area for a bit and discuss the price. If we have a trade-in, we can say, "Well folks, I'll work with you on the price, but since we have a trade-in, let's see how the total picture looks by leaving the list price where it is for simplicity" or, "as it will come up in the computer so we can see what the bottom line is, and then we can work on the total difference. Fair enough?"

Since our offer sheets vary, I will refer to "the proper place on your company's worksheet. Now's where you pull your hit figure (starting number on the trade-in) out of memory, and put it in the proper place on the worksheet. Here again, the words you use are the key to making this a smooth process for maximum profit. Say we have $38,500.00 in the price area and the hit figure you were given by the desk manager was $19,500.00. Now if you had been privy to seeing the actual estimated value of $25,000.00, and you were told to hit 'em at nineteen five, you couldn't pull it off could you? That's why you aren't told what the value may turn out to be after it's appraised; so you can be convincing. I should mention here that you shouldn't give your customer too much credit for their knowledge, and don't think for a minute that they'll know the real value of their trade. They don't. That's the reason we test the water. We can always give more if we have to, but that comes later on. Again, if you have a printed offer form, you simply go line by line.

Now, in the trade-in area, we need the *hit figure*. An easy way to deliver it is, "Folks, when I was in the sales office, I took a peek in our trade book where we keep a record of all vehicles we take in. Not the trade allowances, but the actual true value of the vehicles, and I noticed the last time we took in a car similar to yours, it was stocked in for nineteen thousand five hundred dollars; is that what you had in mind?" Write it down as you ask it. This approach is simple, straightforward, no beating around the bush and non-confrontational. Now, had you sat down and said, "We can give you nineteen thousand five hundred dollars for your trade," that may have ended any chance of further negotiations, wouldn't it? Since you *have not* made that offer, and referred only to another vehicle, and not theirs, your question will be answered without an argument. We expect the customer to object. Everything we do is asking for the maximum profit, and if the customer rolls over and accepts one of our trial closes, we either make a huge profit, or find out they escaped from the psychiatric ward. Quite often in stores where we used computer generated offer forms, I would use this manual method instead whenever I was just discussing figures. It's a lot different when a customer has made a commitment to buy, but in in this case, we are "backing into a commitment."

There are many ways to deliver the hit figure. Some stores have you say, "I asked a senior salesperson," or, "If I remember right, the last time we took in a trade similar to yours," etc. The main thing we want to do is establish our price in the customer's mind, look for objections, trial close the trade allowance, and basically that's what we are doing. That's right, we're getting all the no's out and what's going to follow? Lots and lots of yeses.

I personally like to refer to the *record book of all trades*. This has some credibility, and if the reaction is that it's ridiculous in the customer's mind and they angrily respond; our out is that, "Its condition must not have been as nice as yours." Or, "If I remember right, I think that other car had a lot more miles on it." You may be wondering, "Why it can't be like; here's ours, here's yours and here are the numbers." Now you sound like a customer. The reason we don't lay it all out up front is because we like money. Not only that, but in this method of constructing a write-up, you never lay out an offer that will give you a yes or no without room for negotiating. We are *trial closing* without risking the customer being offended by a direct offer. Now remember, I am showing you how to create an offer from scratch (the hard way). If your store has a computer generated worksheet (offer form), then you will be coming out with that formal proposal. However we do it, we are still working with a shopper that we somehow need to turn into a buyer!

If we make it like walking into a restaurant, and hand them a menu, then the prices would all end up being the lowest, and the trade allowances would be the highest and I'd may as well be back to selling cars through the aid of a German shepherd with a note around his neck. I like to use that example, because I know that I could easily send a German shepherd out to greet customers, and the note would ask them to make their offer and give it to the dog to fetch it back. You will be paid the big bucks if you learn to do this job well. Remember, you were hired in lieu of the Shepherd.

Now, let's see what happens when we hit this customer with $19,500.00 for their trade. *Of* course they'll object, and sometimes forcefully. Maybe mad and loud, "What? Are you nuts? That's crazy!" Don't panic. People react in different ways, and you must always stay calm and remind the customer that, "We haven't even had your car appraised yet." Sometimes you have to raise your voice to even be heard and to bring the customer back to earth. be cool, and say, "Don, don't worry, that was the last one we took in, and I'm sure it wasn't as nice as yours, but I was curious as to whether that was what you felt yours was worth, for my own information." Justify why you hit that number and diffuse the situation. It's as if you are only curious and not even offering anything to them. Remind them that your number is not an offer, because they said they are only curious about the figures.

At this juncture, we are probing the customer for reactions and trying to lower their expectations. We use a hit figure to plant a seed and test the water, but the real appraisal will come back as an exact number. We are simply setting the stage for the next act. The hit figure will normally be lower than the appraisal will come back at, so the buyer will have a pleasant surprise once we enter into actual negotiations.

A relaxing statement at this point will be, "Don't worry about that right now, once your car has been appraised, I'm sure you'll be happy with the numbers." Generally, the customer has tossed out what he wants for his trade-in, and it's advisable that you not write it down. We don't want it written down as a demand, as then, whatever happens when we counter, we must cross out his offer and we're then taking something away from him. It's never a good idea to take away. Better to give more than the number that you wrote down than to cut the number they wrote down. Never write theirs down.

I always told my salespeople to not worry about the customer's reaction to the trade allowance hit figure, but if it was a key point of contention and of *major* importance to the buyer, then to circle it for me. When I came in to close the sale, if I saw a circled trade-in figure, I knew automatically that I had to concentrate on the trade allowance more than the other factors. If it was not circled, I worked the whole deal on monthly payments and brushed over the trade allowance, as it works best in order for us to make the most profit. This is where a close working relationship between salesperson and manager can be the key to success. Most customers will not fight you on the trade figure if the payments work out for them.

Next, we will need to find out how much down payment the customer is prepared to make. This is important. We have a saying in the car business that *cash is profit.* The more cash down you can get, the higher the profit we can make. Think of it this way: Let's say that a customer gives us the amount of monthly payment he will agree to, and we can make that goal with $1,000.00 cash down; and at that, we realize a profit of $500.00. If however, we can convince this customer to put $3,000.00 cash down to hit that same payment, we can roll that extra $2,000.00 straight to profit and make $2,500.00.

Most buyers are payment buyers. By this, I mean they have a budget allocated for their payment that they will buy at. Keep the payments where they can handle them, and they don't care much about trade, price or anything else. Sure, they'll put up a fight like a bass coming to the net, but it's more for the show and the obligatory negotiations, but hit their payment comfort zone, and they'll jump into the boat. This is why they will give you all the down payment money they can in order to meet a payment they can handle. That's why I will repeat; cash is profit! A lot of customers will come in and say, if you can keep my payments where I'm comfortable, I'll buy a car. You get enough of this type of customer, and you'll know there is a Santa Claus. This where the old statement comes from; "The payment buyer is God's gift to the car dealer."

So now we go on, and you say, "Well folks, as you know (they don't know," but by paying them a compliment assuming they are knowledgeable they won't contest your statement), "most lenders require one-third cash down. Based on these figures, we should be looking at (mentally calculate approximately one third of the list price) about thirteen thousand (⅓ of 40,000 list price), can you handle that okay?" At this point, you may run into a myriad of objections, and expect them. They may take many forms such as:

- Customer: "What about the value of our trade-in doesn't that count?"
- Salesperson: "Oh yes but, banks like to see that third down in cash."
- Customer: "Our bank doesn't need any money down."
- Salesperson: "That's good, but in case they may need something, how much would be possible?"

You can see where this could get confusing, so don't over complicate it; get a number that they could use for cash down, and write it down. The customer has likely done this a lot before, so they know the drill. They'll give you a number.

Your dealership may now want you to calculate the approximate payment. Here, I should remind you that this training is upper level, in the respect that most stores will have a shorter track, and you won't get into this for a long time in most stores, and maybe never. But if everyone stayed home and only you and your manager showed up for work, you could sell cars without missing a beat. If they want you to use this system, you will spend many hours training, so this is to give you an idea of one way to do it.

Let's take a look at what we have next; only *the most important part in most transactions.* The payment comes in at this point. Take a look at what we have:

- We have a price of $38,500.00.
- A trade allowance (hit figure) of $19,500.00 (mentally round it to $20,000.00).
- Let's say the customer said he still owes $10,000.00 on the trade.
- You were able to get them to agree to a cash down payment of 4,000.

We need to mentally calculate 38,500 minus 20,000 equals 18,500, adding back in the 10,000 still owing and subtracting the 4,000 leaves us a balance to finance of $24,500.00 doesn't it? Don't worry about anything other than rough numbers. We want to again test the water by "suggesting a payment." Whatever balance you have, mentally round it to a number you can simplify for calculation and multiply it by 3. In this case, think 25,000, so 25 x 3 = 75. An approximate payment will then be $750.00.

So you tell the customers, "Okay Tom, Jane, based on these figures; we should be looking at a payment around $800.00. Can you handle that okay?" Yes, I always round up a bit for wiggle room. The customer will object. Expect it. Say they tell you, "That's too high." Instead of asking what payment they want (it'll always be lower than you need), say, "Well you could handle about $750.00 couldn't you?" Upon receiving another objection; your final question should be, "Tom, Jane, let me ask you this; how close to $750.00 could you come, and still buy the car right now?" and write it down. Now, all you have to do is recap what you have. "So folks, what you're telling me then is, if we can take your car in trade, four thousand cash down, and keep your payments at $650.00 a month, you'll buy the car and drive it home now, right? Okay, go ahead and sign here and I'll present your offer." Have them sign it. If they won't, then recap, and ask again. You need a commitment. You have likely been already taught to not use the word *sign*. Most trainers tell you to ask them to "O.K." the figures, and that's all right to do, I like to use the word sign. It's stronger and works better. I want the strongest commitment I can get. I understand that people tend to fear saying sign to anyone; this is my personal quirk because it is powerful and I don't like to take too much time to get serious.

This may have seemed like a complicated scenario, but in actuality, it only takes about fifteen minutes. Once they have agreed to buy and made the offer, set the offer to the side, open up your customer statement (credit application), and start filling it out. You already have their names and address, phone number, and the basics. Now here, you can take the application in an hour or you can do it in fifteen minutes. You will be taught that by law, the customer is supposed to fill out the application themselves. This is the one hour version. My version is to explain this to the customer, and I say; "Now if you'd like, since I know what is needed, I'll be glad to fill it in for you, and you can sign it; okay?" This is my 15 minute version; first of all, when you're taking a credit application or any other information from a customer, any time there is a silence, it creates an uncomfortable lull, and they will feel compelled to break the silence by asking a question. When they do, it will be unnecessary, and take time, so here's what you do, and don't change it. *Talk the app.* That's correct, ask a question, and when they answer, repeat it as you write. Now ask your next question, and then talk it. If you keep asking questions, talking and writing, you'll get done in less than half the time, and time is precious. Once you have the app filled out, signed and dated, then offer a refreshment refill, and take your paperwork to the office.

Now, if you want a one hour version, hand the app to them, go away, and come back later on. They'll not only have a lot of questions, but it will be messed up. If you are not in control of the questioning process, then they will make errors that can kill your deal. Take the income portion where it asks for monthly earnings; the customer who has $500.00 a month sent directly to savings may forget to include it in his monthly income because he doesn't count it as spendable income, and he only puts down what he actually sees on his check. That may stop him from qualifying for a loan because you weren't there to explain the question. This happens a lot. Many customers don't even understand the difference between gross and net income.

When you're new, someone else (closer or sales manager) will be coming out now to present the dealership's offer, and you will need to make a polite introduction and then sit there and keep your mouth shut. Always keep absolutely quiet, and never, ever say a single word unless asked by your manager.

There are many sales managers and dealers around the country who still bear the memory of being kicked by me under the table in their early careers as salesmen when they spoke out of turn. I remember at a big dealer group meeting one day when the general manager of a large dealership came up and shook my hand, and said, "I still remember you kicking me, and you always wore those exotic cowboy boots. I can still feel it, but I learned a valuable lesson." He obviously did well.

Believe me when I say, speaking when someone is closing your deal is grounds for termination in a lot of stores. It is probably the worst possible thing you can do. I have sat for as long as half an hour after asking a closing question without anyone speaking. Then the customer reached out and shook my hand. Think about it. A half hour of silence; a man and wife, my salesperson and me. The couple passing a calculator and notes back and forth, and me counting holes in the ceiling. Finally a deal. Had I rephrased the question or spoken at all, the pressure would have been off and I'd have lost.

Write this down, or etch it in your brain — After asking a closing question, the first one who talks, loses. I've had customers even say, "This is a lot of pressure." I do not reply, I smile and keep my mouth shut. If they break the silence with some kind of question, then I answer it, and rephrase the buying question, or ask another one and then I again shut up. Think about the poor salesmen I kicked. Not only did they have painful shins, but they most likely also lost a sale, because they talked first and lost.

To all those people, I do not apologize, because they learned a lesson that some salesmen never do. No, I never had to kick a lady. They seem to learn faster, although I do remember having to nudge their shoes slightly, or giving them a look that could kill.

I know we went through this manual method of constructing an offer to purchase rather quickly, but my intention is to give you a glimpse into a system that while not largely used anymore, it was the mainstay of the car business that began in the eastern United States, then to Indianapolis, and jumped out to the west coast. It was called the Hull-Dobbs System, and it went so far as to hide trades, throw car keys on roofs, and they pulled every crooked scheme you could imagine. When you wonder why people don't trust you, it's because your predecessors earned the reputation that you have to live with. I could write volumes on the dishonest and ultra-sleazy methods, but it's best to let the past fade away.

Most of today's systems will be a lot easier than the manual, do it all from scratch method we discussed; so let's examine some others. This method is a more casual and seemingly innocent way of backing into a transaction. More modern presentations have been created to continually upgrade the selling process. I have worked with a great number of computer generated offers and they are a lot easier to present. The basic figures that the desk manager enters are the same numbers as the manual method, so the numbers don't change, only our ways of presenting them. You at least have an idea of what can always be done if your computers all die and you have to learn to write and think for yourself.

In most cases, a sales manager will take the same basic information on the vehicle you're selling; the trade data, and based on the credit score of the customer, will be able to print out a proposal. The proposal is then shown to the customer and the dealing begins. The problem with this method is that the customer is asked for permission to run his credit, and this involves taking the customer statement before we have earned the right by first discussing numbers. You lose some this way, such as the "I'm just looking" crowd; and that's a big crowd. As I said, the manual method backs into a sale by never directly making the customer an offer. You make trial closes and suggestions, but you never confront your customer with an offer up front. Do it only *after* setting the stage.

In this other method, you may advertise a new way of doing business, and dealers do. They go to great lengths to blast the media with a no obligation, "We show you the figures up front, and let you make the decision." The preliminaries are the same. You still go through the same process. The difference is that you don't have the same script.

Once you take the initial paperwork to the desk manager, they will print out a proposal. Now your job is to present the numbers to your buyer. It will have the figures all neatly printed. The selling price, trade allowance, payoff on trade, and payment and lease options will be shown. Many of these proposals will give many options for payments based on cash down, and many options on terms. Most of these proposals also have a section of lease options. If you are selling a used vehicle, there will not generally be a lease option.

This plan is similar to the manual write-up in that we show the customer a proposal, and he reacts to it. No major difference except in this more direct form, you don't need to ease into the agreement. You make a proposal, and you get an immediate reaction. You therefore must know how to react, and be prepared to do it quickly if your customer balks, or reacts by getting to his feet. You may have to swiftly diffuse the situation, and it never hurts to quickly react to a strong negative pushback. I should mention that the degree of reaction from the buyer is determined by how the numbers are presented. The higher the profit the manager is trying for, the tougher job you may have, but the more money you will make. Stay strong, and if the manager asks how much control you have, say, "Hit me hard." In other words, always ask for the highest profit and be strong. "You don't ask, you won't get!"

I may, if the customer reacts strongly, say, "Bill, keep in mind that this proposal is the best case for us, but what do you feel would be the best case for you?" Now, he will sit back down, and show you exactly what you need to do in order to earn his business. Keeping in mind that he gave you his best case deal; he knows that he's being overly optimistic, and you need to remind him of this. You can say something like, "Okay Bill, this is best for you, and this other one is best for my boss, so where do you think we can get together in between?" As you ask this, follow up with a *split the difference offer* of some kind. Not an even split, but something close to what your initial proposal presented. So if your trade allowance was $11,000.00

and the customer says he will accept $18,000.00; you should ask him if he will trade for an allowance of $12,000.00. That's a split. If he challenges me by, "You asked me if I'd split the difference. $12,000 is not a split." I'll say, "I didn't say an even split," (with a big smile).

Your job now is to get all the price, cash down, the least amount he will take for the trade-in; but remember the trade allowance is usually not of major importance to the customer, so don't sit there and argue it. Ask the important question, "So Bill, what you're telling me is (recap what he had agreed to), and if we can do all that, you'll buy the car and drive it home now, right?" Now, you take the offer to the sales office, and you are back in the same position you were with the manual method. In this method, you only have to deliver the numbers, get all you can from the buyer and turn it in. You see, there is nothing complicated in selling cars. You offer, get the customer's offer, and present it to management. While you're negotiating, you must be aware of his "hot button." Is he pushing you hard on the trade allowance to lower his payment? If so, concentrate on cash down and payment and stay away from trade allowance. I have many times stated it like this, "Johnny, if I could get you the payment you're asking for, I could probably give you a hundred dollars for trade; couldn't I?" They most always answered, "Yes." This is how payment buyers think.

SETUP AND INTRO TO THE CLOSER

Whenever a manager is to be involved, a proper setup is mandatory. You must be careful of the relationship that you have established with your customers and everything you do must have a benefit to them. You cannot afford any surprises. Surprises in a car deal are disastrous. I can always picture the shocked look on customer's faces when other closers suddenly appeared with a loud, "Hi folks, I'm John Dillinger the manager," and sat down. No setup, unannounced, and unwelcome. Don't ever pull these surprises on your customers.

When you have a written offer, handle it like this; "Mr. and Mrs. Customer, when my boss hired me, he told me that if I ever needed any help, I only needed to ask. Well, looking at these numbers that you want, I would sure feel a lot more comfortable having my boss present your offer to our sales manager. He has a lot more clout than I do, so if it's all right with you, I'd like to ask him to join us? His name is Gary Swanson and he's a great guy." Of course your customers will be all for it, because they feel that you have their best interests at heart. Now you depart to turn in your paperwork. When the closer comes to your table, immediately stand up (even if you have left a chair for him) and make your introductions. Show your closer respect, because you need your customers to feel that he is an important person to you and not another salesperson playing a role as boss. This happens way too often and should never be done at all. Customers can tell the difference between a sales manager and your fellow salesperson simply by your body language!

I hope you understand that this show of respect is necessary to make your manager's arrival something special. The two of you work together to help your buyers get the best deals they could ever imagine. This method of introduction to the manager, and this showing of such respect, was not of my teaching. My sales teams did this of their own accord, and customers ate it up. I always felt that my teams overdid it, but it worked so well that I can't argue with such tremendous success.

GET OUT OF JAIL FREE

Customers are afraid of car people! First of all, the average customer who works a boring occupation (most anything other than ours) is not used to someone suddenly jumping in their face and asking 20 questions. Therefore, when he or she drives on to our lot, they are apprehensive; sometimes to a point of being downright hostile!

I have worked in many major cities where the majority of dealerships were dog-eat-dog, what they called "system houses," you know, those almost kill or be killed dealers to scare your grandchildren with. Any customers who had visited one of those type stores were often visibly afraid when being approached by our salespeople!

You can tell right off if you get one of these customers, as you'll likely be met with, "Can't we just look by ourselves?" They'll almost be yelling at you. I love these types of buyers, because I'll sell every one of them!

Assuming that these people will already be on the lot somewhere, because they commonly drive straight toward the service department, parts or body shop, without so much as a glance at the inventory. Then they will find the first vacant spot to park and stealthily sneak around into the inventory without being noticed by the salespeople who are all watching the entrances for the next *live one*.

I always enjoyed these types of people, because if you get them to like you, it's an automatic sale! My approach would be along the lines of, "Oh, hello folks, have you been helped yet?" Their general response would be from, "We've already been helped," to, "We don't want any help!" to, "Can't we look around without being pressured?" and many, even more defiant.

My own response would be a happy smile and then, "Of course you can. If you give me an idea of what you may be looking for, I'd be happy to point out where they are, and then I'll get out of your way so you can be free to help yourself." Some innocuous statement that would lead the people into new, used, or whatever, but they are never very specific. Then after they would maybe say "used cars," I'd respond by pointing some out, hopefully with me walking them toward the area, and then I'd add, "We also have many fresh trade-ins that are in various stages of being serviced, and if you don't find something you like, just wave me over and I can let you know what else we have. I'll be over there," and I'll gesture to a place a ways off.

Now, I'll turn as if to depart, and then I say, "If you have any questions, give me a nod. Oh; allow me to give you my business card so if anyone else asks, simply tell them you're with me. Meanwhile, I'll keep the wolves away!" Then I walk away out of earshot to give them the privacy as I promised. No, save the actual intro for later!

Think about what I have done; I have established the fact I respect their privacy by not pushing for their names, I have acknowledged that they think of us as a "pack of wolves," I positioned myself to give them space, and I gave them their *get out of jail free* card.

Within a couple of minutes, almost every time, these people will call me over after they see if I'll keep my word, and they will always ask some simple question with which to break the ice. Which I will answer, and *again* I'll turn to leave, and they'll ask me another question, which at this point, I now take the lead. I introduce myself, I write their names on a business card, give each of them my card again, and we're off and running! I will sell most every single one of these people on the spot. Also, they will happily pay all the money and end up being fantastic repeat buyers for years to come! Plus that, they generally have a group of close friends with similar distaste of car people, and I'll sell them also. Note: You notice I said I will give these people my cards again; in case the first ones were tossed. Also, I print their names (verifying spelling and pronunciation) on my own card. I never used pre-printed prospect cards; I need to be informal!

You will always be their "only friend in the business." Treat them like royalty whenever they come in, and when they send in their friends do the same. Many of these people will actually drive in with friends to personally make the introductions, and then when their friends are comfortable with you, they will depart.

When they bring in or refer someone you sell, remember to call them later and send them a "thank you" gift or cash. Never forget this! Build your "owner file" and in a few years you may never have a need to work the floor again. If you can, it's better to deliver a *bird dog* gift in person.

Many shoppers will drop a casual remark that they have a "friend in the business," simply say, "Now you have another one." Then continue on, because people will buy from the devil himself if they feel they can save money.

Occasionally, but thankfully not too often, a customer will test your honesty by suddenly deviating from what they've been looking at and switch to some W.T. (wretched turd) that's totally opposite from what you have been showing them. Or, maybe some outlandishly pricey 2-door sporty model that is a total departure from what they really need. This is just a "test" to see if you throw all caution to the wind and try to upgrade them so your commission will be greater. Don't be alarmed, it's normal. They're reinforcing their opinion of your honesty, so stay on track.

We also must be careful to stay within the parameters we established upon our first meeting them.

You notice that I always print their names on my card, and as I do, I ask for the *spellings* with a comment on how "their names are important to me!"

When you keep it casual, from this point on, you'll notice they will glance at your card periodically before calling you by name. They will appreciate the courtesy of separate cards. This is your best investment!

SELL THE APPRAISAL TO YOUR CUSTOMER

Over my career, I purchased millions of dollars' worth of used cars from auto auctions, but the best source of used cars are the ones traded in at our dealership on new purchases by customers.

So it seems that across the country, the normal procedure is for structuring an offer to the buyer based on less than the appraised value as determined by the used car manager. Naturally we offer *less* than the appraisal, because if we can get the customers to accept a thousand or two less than the *actual cash value* of their vehicle (what it's really worth), that turns directly into gross profit which increases the commissions! You can have a direct effect on this appraisal.

Let's think about that for a minute; while we are telling the customer what their trade-in is worth, they each have their own thoughts about their car, but neither person is ready to accept such a low amount as we offer for trade-in value. So what have we missed? *The biggest money maker ever!*

Before we discuss any numbers, we need to *sell* the appraisal. Here's how; the salesperson must keep the customers with them while filling out the appraisal sheet. Have the customers there to help read you the VIN (vehicle identification number), mileage, and whatever else while you inspect the vehicle *together!*

Our purpose is to *sell* the appraisal; which they have yet to see. What we are doing is lowering the customer's expectations. By involving them in the vehicle appraisal, the salesperson needs to reach down and run a finger over the scratch on the back door, as if trying to see how bad it is. Also, the rock chips on the hood, the star in the windshield, stains in the seats from kids and dogs, the scratch on the hood where Mom set the baby seat to change Junior.

We need to put a coin in the tire tread to check the depth of the remaining tread, we need to notice the dark spots in the front carpet where the soft drinks spilled at various times; we can go on and on, but you have the idea. Everything we touch is lowering the customer's expectations.

It is quite common for people to forget all of the things that happen during their ownership of vehicles. In today's hectic lifestyle, these items add up, and when pointed out to a customer, or silently and visibly indicating those items that diminish the vehicle's value, they will now be less apt to argue about the vehicle's value. This is how you *sell the appraisal* without saying a word! Believe me; this can be the easiest and best moneymaker over anything else, and you don't have to say a word!

This silent appraisal does so much to reduce the customer's expectations that one can easily pick up several thousand dollars of additional profit by a few minutes of *silently selling the appraisal.* Multiply your commission percentage times this amount, times all of the trades you average in a month, and now multiply that figure by 12. Quite a substantial year-end bonus isn't it!

This trade-in procedure should be used in all dealerships, and I am surprised when I see operations that do not use this procedure. It's a silent salesperson working with you to build gross profit!

Notes on selling the vehicle itself; I do not wish to suggest changing any procedures in force in your store, but a couple of thoughts on my preferences. I never liked the idea of presenting a vehicle on the lot; there are way too many interruptions and distractions. I like to select the vehicle; I drive first, then pulling into my favorite spots to do my complete presentation. These spots are business parking lots on weekends when they are closed, churches during weekdays, city parks, just pick a few favorites.

Now we go on our test drive; and please make sure if there are two customers, both buyers drive the vehicle. Do your very best to get both people to drive; it's really a great help anytime you are working with a couple, to keep both of them involved in the decision making. Never forget to try very hard to make them both drive; it's critical!

NO SNEAKING UP

Whatever method your dealership uses for you to meet a customer, make certain that they see you approaching. You must approach in a manner that they see you coming, and never come up on them from behind, or you'll scare hell out of them; you may as well *turn* them right away! Startle a customer and you embarrass them. At that point go stick a fork in yourself, because you are done!

Scuff your feet, make some noise, pretend you are waving to someone; anything to alert them to your presence. I liked to loudly say, "Thanks folks," and when the people I was approaching turned to look at me, I'd be waving at invisible customers, but I'd immediately be turning back and I would then greet them without having embarrassed them at all. Very important!

SOURCES OF BUSINESS – COURTESIES TO REMEMBER

Let's talk BDC; Business Development Center.

It's funny that the automobile dealers waited so long to professionalize their biggest source of customers; the "call-ins." People who are shopping by phone for particular vehicles, responding to TV or newspaper ads, or just going through the phone book.

The BDC teams are sequestered in a quiet phone room where they work hard to convince those callers to visit the dealership. These pleasant people are trained to relax the caller and they "sell" the caller on making an appointment.

Many customers are genuinely afraid to drive on to a car lot and be chased by a half dozen aggressive young salespeople. Then when they stop, there's a smiling dimwit at both doors. That kind of activity would scare a mountain man.

I had the pleasure of setting up one of the first BDC's in Portland, Oregon, and it really showed us how professional we could really be! The BDCs will bring the customer in, and if you're smart, you will cultivate these people working in the phone room.

When you make a sale because of a phone appointment from one of these people, a $20 bill goes a long way toward that person seeing that you get another one directed right to you (even though they are not supposed to) if you're subtle about it. Gratuities are always appreciated, and anyone who causes you to make money should always be acknowledged with a perk.

This is a courtesy that is largely disappearing now days, however, in the past, dealers always had "bird dog" lists that salespeople were encouraged to use and keep. For example, some clerk in a store you frequent spots your nametag and sends his uncle to you and the uncle buys a new truck from you. Your commission is $2,100! Do you think it might be worth dropping off some business cards to that clerk and maybe a Franklin ($100 bill; and make it a new looking bill) as a thank you? That may be all it takes for a serious raise in your income, because this kid may hand out your cards more often than you do. Make sure he puts his name on them!

CULTIVATE YOUR CUSTOMER BASE

As our business has grown more sophisticated, many of the old techniques have gone away, however, you must remember you are not a sheep! The most successful people in sales do no sit around and wait for *ups* to stream in the door; they constantly work to create a more reliable stream of business from every source they can!

Don't concentrate on only being a "floor whore!" There are always those aggressive salespeople who do not care who they jump in front of to get the next customer. They never make phone calls (prospecting); they never respect others and will cut you off and step in front of you at every chance. Aggressive beyond reason? Perhaps; however, if they are good at what they do, they are likely making a lot of money. Do you expect their supervisor to even think of pulling them back?

There is often a slight difference between being aggressive or being rude. Try not to be too sensitive. If you work at a store where the first one to greet the customer gets them, taking turns is the last courtesy you can expect.

When a sales manager's income depends on his team of salespeople, do not expect him to even ask the aggressive salesperson to take it easy. To the contrary; he or she would like to have an entire sales team as aggressive!

Personally, I hated the times I worked in dealerships with rotating systems when all teams were on the sales floor together. Reason being, I wanted my team to get *every* up! Fortunately, I seldom had to worry about it, because the rules were soon changed (of course, at my insistence)!

I am courteously aggressive! I hope you will be also. My rule, or call it a very strong suggestion, is that when all teams worked the same shifts (weekends); no salesperson in the dealership should have a customer until my team were all working with customers!

You may now have the thought that this seems like a hard condition to work under, but think about it; the retail car business is a *lazy* career. The reason is primarily that we make more money than most people, and it comes with such little effort it can have an adverse effect on many salespeople. Most salespeople are not born in this business; we came from other occupations where we were expected to work our complete shifts, with regulated breaks.

Suddenly we are exposed to the car biz where the money is super, we can goof-off whenever, and if not watched carefully by our superiors; we can easily fail! That's right, we've all seen the hero to zero syndrome. I could never let this happen to my team, because they were not allowed to fail!

Look at it this way; you come in to this *fun* business where you dress well, spend the majority of your time out of the weather, can sit around and chat with your associates, and most likely make two to four times what you ever earned before.

You soon buy a new car, a new home, and you're on "Easy Street." Great! As I said, this is a lazy business. With all of your major purchases come major payments and major obligations. The danger I spoke of is that you perhaps earned it too quickly, and many car people are like a speedboat with the huge wake running close behind it. If the boat stops suddenly, say hello to a wall of water!

Newcomers to our business often get hit with that wall of water. Not because they ran out of gas, but because their lifestyle has changed so dramatically, they weren't prepared for such prosperity.

Often they do it to themselves; they start *running*, heading to the bar after work, chasing with other people, going home drunk, having car accidents, and showing up late for work sporting a hangover. Soon the family falls apart and your luxurious and fun lifestyle goes down the tube!

I never allowed this to happen to my sales teams, and if you are a manager take note.

MANAGERS – TREAT YOUR JOB WITH RESPECT

Anytime you are responsible for the success or failure of a sales team, the example you set will determine all of your futures. The rules that follow are what I learned by watching other managers fail in their duties.

My sales teams were always in first place in every dealership I worked at. Yes, I had a lot of jobs and I made lots of money and worked long hours; so periodically, I needed a vacation. No, two weeks just couldn't cut it; I needed a month or three! Coming back I often went to the same store and often changed franchises for more excitement. Yes, I took a lot of my people with me. No bragging, just discussing work ethics.

Rules for managers:

> Always be early to work. You should be there first and leave last. You should never be there after your salespeople have already arrived!

> Set two alarm clocks. Have a backup clock set 10 minutes after the first one.

➤ Never allow your sales team to be late. A good way to correct tardiness is every time a person is late in a month, go to the sales board and erase a letter of their first name. I've used this and it works well. If their name is gone before the month's end, so are they!

➤ Don't party with your sales team after work. You are not a member of the fun club; you are the leader!

➤ Do not allow cellphones to be used during work hours. Designated call times only (see the Cellphones chapter). You follow the rules also!

➤ Spend your days on your feet; preferably where your salespeople watch for ups.

➤ Set incentives from you to them; such as treating them to the casino with dinner and some gambling money if they make top crew. Yes, we were; 12 times a year! Thanks for asking.

These may seem like harsh rules, but you are not only there to earn an excellent income for yourself, but every one of your salespeople and their families depend directly on you for their livelihood! That's why it's called management.

MAY I OFFER YOU SOME REFRESHMENTS?

All dealerships have a section where the coffee machines, soda dispensers and candy concessions live. Many of the stores offer them free (at least coffee), but this can be one of your *most important* sales aids!

Whenever you have brought customers in to your showroom and seated them at a table to talk business, set the stage. After they have been seated, they most always will ask to use the restrooms. This is a good indication that they are willing to discuss business and they want to be relaxed.

Before they depart for the facilities, you ask, "May I get you a cup of coffee or a soda?" At this exact point, you will set a very important obligation into effect! Reach into your pocket and pull out some money. Use a money clip (best) or just some green cash; and this must be done so they can see the bills as you offer! This simple gesture will cement an obligation for the customer to allow you all the time you need to present and discuss your proposal. You've heard of "buying time!" Just the showing of the cash and your offer will greatly enhance your chances to sell. In addition to your generosity, people will not leave until they finish their drink. You bought the time, so use it to sell a car!

THE BUYING PROCESS

I will not get into my own selling techniques, as they may conflict with your manager's teaching, but one thing you will need to do at this point is to ascertain whether or not you have a "buyer," and if so, if they will buy *now*!

Where it has not been made apparent by the customer, or if I detect that they fear what is coming next (they know we're not here to entertain guests), is to determine their timetable. It's easy to lean back from the table and ask, "So, Chip, Dale, where do you think you're at in the buying process; the beginning, the middle, or the end?"

So they answer, "The middle." You now have the non-pushy opportunity to ask, "And why do you say the middle?" Now you can go to work and get them to the end. This could end up being the most expensive cup of coffee they ever received for free!

If you're new to the profession, it's kind of a fake it till you make it proposition. Never lie to a customer! You may stretch the living hell out of the truth, but no direct lies!

Something I do not believe in and I feel you should never do is play games! The old adversarial operation of "It's us against the house," does not work in modern sales negotiations.

The boss is not the bad guy. His job is to make sure to sell every vehicle he can, and to earn enough money to keep the doors open, but he's on your and your customer's side. The good guy-bad guy garbage should never be used!

In addition, let your buyers know that they can't pay too much for a vehicle, because the factory sets the prices, and thanks to the United States Senator Monroney, the stickers are regulated by law. Competition keeps the manufacturers in line also.

What I enjoy doing a lot of times after I explain that to people, is to look them in the eye and say, "So because of that, I'll have to *steal* your trade-in!" Then we all have a good laugh and I make money. You can see my style of selling is to keep it fun; always.

DRESS CODE

There are many opinions out there on proper dress for salespeople; I believe mine are the best, and since you paid for mine, thanks. Here they are!

Many so-called experts say to dress down to not appear to be making too much money. First of all, there is no such thing as too much money; secondly, that opinion stinks!

Do you want your customers to believe you are not making money? You seem like a nice person, so maybe the cars you're representing are no good?

I suggest you dress well. You want to give your buyer the impression that you are doing very well. Nobody wants to deal with a loser! Dress as a successful business person would.

Now the ladies on the other hand, must unfortunately dress down a bit. Sounds unfair, doesn't it? Reason being is that you are dealing with a totally different challenge than your male counterpart; the wife!

Picture if you will, the pheasant; the male is beautifully adorned with the finest plumage and he is in charge! The female human is in the same position; beautifully adorned and in charge! So how will she react when she comes in with her husband to look at cars, and out steps a fashion model in a gorgeous outfit, high heels, and enough said! Ladies, dress down to be neat and clean, with flat heels and comfortable clothing. Comfortable for both you and the wife!

Do, by all means, direct the majority of your questions to the wife. This is imperative! This man is not a pheasant. He is married, he is seldom in charge anyway, but don't make the mistake of testing this theory. I truly adhere to my belief that in 90% of all cases, the wife will make the buying decision, and in the other 10%, she "allows" her husband to do so.

For the salesmen your attire is easier, but always make certain to dress like a professional. Get a businesslike haircut. Watch the excess facial hair; no stubble, people know you weren't just rescued from some remote island!

You're representing your dealership and your product. Don't give the appearance of just hopping out of your jammies and coming to work! Check your eyes for those obnoxious "sleep seeds." Periodically visit the restroom mirror for a "checkup from the neck up." Smile!

You should always have shined shoes! When you're on the lot, shoes get dusty; wipe them with a shoe cloth regularly throughout your shift.

Clean clothes and nice appearance are a must. No hiking boots allowed. If you wore them to most stores, you would be told appropriately to, "Go take a hike or change your shoes!" Oh yes, one more very important item, clean and trimmed fingernails are a must!

There are not as many smokers as before, but watch out for *dragon breath*!

These may seem trivial, but you're not selling shoes; you're asking someone to spend many thousands of dollars. Look like you deserve it!

SELLING USED VEHICLES

This is the department that's really fun and sometimes pays a higher commission percentage, but has more going for it than you'd first think.

To begin with, all used vehicles are unique. There are no two exactly alike. The used car buyer will not be as picky about condition as their new car counterpart.

As I mentioned, the commissions may be higher, because you don't have the luxury of selection; also, your new vehicle franchise is what most people come in for, but the main dollar incentive is that the used car pricing is not limited or regulated like the factory determined markup on a new vehicle. The used vehicle will have a much greater profit margin than the new one.

The used vehicle is easier to sell, but you need to spend a lot of time getting familiar with a greater variety of features.

If I were given a choice between selling new vehicles or selling from a well-stocked used car department, I'd pick used every time. Sure, I'd lose the luxury in many cases of hanging around a nicely decorated showroom, and maybe wearing nicer clothes, and a TV somewhere close to check scores of ball games, and soda machines close at hand, and all of those things that many people like. However, if I'm going to spend 8 to 12 hours a day at work, I want to be well-compensated for it! That means used cars.

Look at it this way; no two used cars are identical. Your buyers will not be pointing at every rock chip and try to beat your price down because of it; also the used vehicle will be priced according to the market. Think about the extremely hard to find new vehicle that is the hottest thing going that your used car manager gets a used one out of another market where the demand is not so great; you can likely make a few house payments with your commissions for selling that one!

If you are in used car sales, you know what I mean! Study your product every day and learn the features. The more you learn the more you'll earn, because knowledge plus enthusiasm over the vehicle wins every time!

The more you know about a vehicle, the more your customers will think it is because you do really like it!

NEGOTIATING STRATEGIES THAT WORK FASTER AND BETTER

If a buyer gives you a short objection without a long, drawn out narrative, return the same type of shorter answer. Such as; he says, "That's not nearly enough for my trade allowance." You reply with, "It never is, is it?" This may be all you need to do instead of a long, drawn out defense of your trade appraisal. Your customer may just say with a shrug, "No, but it will work; I'll take it." Expect an objection; that's what buyers are supposed to do, so don't try to defend it. If you tried anything else in this example, you likely would be in for a few more passes, but trying a non-defensive strategy works well!

Customers don't like to make major arguments and quite often they will offer a "token" resistance, but you must resist the temptation to jump to the defense of your offer. Sit quiet, smile, and let the offer you presented sell itself. Remember the old two ears and one mouth theory that suggest we listen twice as much as we talk! Besides, if you rush in to respond, you are not answering a question, you are reacting to his or her statement, and you are on the defensive.

Most salespeople will jump in like that to offer more defense of our offer when they should be sitting with a polite smile and keep their mouths shut! Silence sells! Stop running back and forth. Sit there, shut your mouth, smile and don't move!

Quite often, out of sheer nervousness and the fear of losing a sale, we try too hard. You must always keep foremost in your mind that you do this for a living and you have to be here. Your customer does not! He's here because he wants to own a vehicle which you own. Therefore, stop running back and forth like your buyer's bird dog and sit there and be calm.

You will usually reach a point where your buyer will let out a gasp of imitating his best interpretation of exhaust and maybe even more emphatic, and he says in a steady, calm tone, "Go tell your boss that I'll make one final offer. Tell him to give me another thousand dollars for my trade and I'll do it."

You know there's room to do it, and you heard your sales manager's boss say to him quietly, "You're on board, get all you can and roll it." So you know at this point you have a sale, now you need to calm down and make a bonus! What you have at stake is your commission on that $1,000.00 your customer is asking for. $200 to $250 is usually what your participation would cost you personally if your boss made that entire $1,000 concession. So keep your butt in the chair, your feet on the floor and close the sale!

Yes, it's your commission at stake, and you can always retreat to the sales office or you can put on your most sincere look and try this. Look your customer directly at the spot between his eyes, lean forward and reply, "Jim, I wish I could do it for you, but the last time I was in the office, I heard my general manager tell my boss that at those figures (gesture to your offer sheet), we're all in." Your customer will be looking at you and then at the sheet. *At that exact time* he looks down at the sheet, slowly reach out your hand and quietly, but so you can be heard, ask, "Can we go ahead and do it?" He *will* shake your hand! Do that every time and you'll dramatically raise your pay checks. In 80 percent of all cases, he will shake your hand! In the other instances, you make the trip to the office.

Remember, your buyers don't like the offer-counter offer process any more than you do, but every pass is *making* you money and *costing* them money. So if anybody is having fun, it should be you!

Now if you should get into one of those embarrassing situations where your hand is stretched out in anticipation of a shake, what happens if your buyer just sits there without reacting? Yes, I have experienced a few of these situations where the person didn't even twitch an eyebrow. You must remember that when having asked a closing question, "The first one who talks loses." This includes pulling back an aching hand!

This however, has a further complication; the pain in the outstretched arm gets steadily worse! You know if you pull your arm back, it's like retracting your *closing question*, so you can't do that. I have many times had to carefully and slowly bring my left hand up and support my outstretched arm. This also becomes painful; believe me, but it works!

In the end, I have never lost one of these actions, but I have endured a lot of pain in doing these moves. When you look at the reality of the situation, the buyer paid me $50 a minute to watch me hold my own arm up for the five minutes. Too bad there isn't a circus act for car guys! Maybe that was it?

YOU CAN NEGOTIATE TOO HARD

I have always negotiated hard, but fairly. However, once, the buyer reminded, me by a very polite lesson, that sometimes winning can go a step too far!

I was negotiating back and forth with a university professor who owned a ranch where he raised expensive show horses for a hobby. We argued our way down to mere dollars, both of us wanting to win, and finally I said, "Okay, throw in two horseshoes for my office wall and we have a deal." We shook on it and I forgot all about that last few dollar bump.

Then about two weeks later, the professor showed up at my store with a package; which I quickly opened. There was a beautiful hat rack he had fashioned out of two horseshoes, so one could be attached to my wall, with ends up in a "U" of course, and welded to the center base, was half of the other shoe to make a beautiful hook to hang my Stetson; which I usually wore.

I was really impressed and thanked him profusely, and as he was leaving, he turned to me with a huge smile and said, "Gary, you notice you only got one and a half horseshoes." All of his effort was such a great and professional way to teach me about limits on negotiating.

I was glad he won! Actually, it was a win-win.

ARE YOU TRYING TO CON ME?

Often when you are into heavy negotiations, situations sometimes can become tense. Tempers can flare on both sides. We must react calmly but quickly to diffuse the situation.

Often the quickest way back to a more cordial atmosphere is to use the shock value of an off the wall response that catches the customer totally off-guard.

For example, let's take the customer who gets annoyed with the negotiations and demands an additional $2,000 for his trade-in. His salesperson offers the thought that he may be able to talk the boss into allowing another one hundred dollars and the buyer comes unglued!

Let's say the buyer gives you the retort of, "Are you trying to con me?" and glares at the salesperson. Many salespeople doing the negotiating may argue for another half hour and never sell a car, so instead I put a quizzical look on my face and answer with, "I just thought I'd try!" Then before he can even fully comprehend, I follow with a chuckle, and we're friends again.

Quite often with certain personalities I have found it to be more a necessity to push the negotiations to a point where they can *unload!* With these types of people, it almost seems as though the pressure of their job and frustrations they have pent up from work stress suddenly explode to the surface. Then, once they blow off steam, their entire persona changes and they're back to being nice people once more. Therefore, never be shocked if they explode!

These personality types are generally in pressure jobs where they deal all week with their employees' problems without being able to release their tension. Once the explosion ends, these people usually become our best customers. They will return time and time again, and bring their friends!

BUSINESS CARDS AND EMAIL ADDRESSES

This is one of your best advertising methods. Hand business cards out wherever you go. Do *not* have your cell number imprinted on them however. That is your opportunity to make someone feel special, by printing your cellphone number on the card you hand them.

Additionally, you want calls coming in on your dealership's landline anyway. Your cellphone and you need to be divorced when you are at work anyway!

Make certain you have an email address on your cards, but no cell number, but don't forget to add it by hand!

REHEARSAL TIME

I hope your sales team rehearses together. Practicing negotiating strategies with teammates is of great value. When you practice on your fellow salespeople and make a mistake, it costs you nothing; whereas if you make the same error with a customer, you lose money. The more you practice negotiating with teammates and your managers, the better you get at your job and the more money you make!

Your dentist practiced drilling and filling on dummies and fake heads for many hours before you walked into his office. You owe it to yourself, your family, and your employer to be the best you can be!

That reminds me of the old example where a man pulls up to a taxi stand in New York and asks, "How do I get to Carnegie Hall?" The cabbie answers, "Practice!"

HOW DO YOUR NUMBERS SOUND?

When your customer asks what their price will be, do you say, "Thirty-nine eight fifty," or "Thirty-nine thousand eight hundred and fifty dollars"? When you are discussing price, be careful to just say it as the *short sound* example.

Always express the customer's trade allowance in a way to make it sound bigger. An example of a trade allowance of $22,500 would never be, "Twenty-two five." Instead, we always say, "Twenty-two thousand, five hundred dollars."

The better your numbers sound, the better the numbers on your paycheck will look!

THAT'S UPSIDE DOWN!

Anytime you can steal or borrow, or even purchase an idea or a technique that you can use to make money; do it. I got this one from the insurance business. In insurance presentations back in the early days, there were no laptops or computers. The entire presentation consisted of a notebook with a step by step series of pages that progressed from the beginning to the final benefit and costs. The pages were covered with acetate and we wrote numbers and words on the plastic pages with an erasable marker. For the maximum effect, we faced the book toward the customers and whether at a table or on a chair facing clients on a couch, the entire presentation was done by writing words and numbers upside down. This way it impressed them, as we weren't constantly turning pages around.

When I got into the retail automobile business, I sometimes found myself doing this on occasion as I was constructing an offer or negotiating. It was often easier while the sheet was facing the buyers for me to cross out a number and write in another one. It got so I did this more and more often and while customers would usually comment on how I did that, I'd answer, "Laziness. I don't have to move the sheet." The reason I continued doing this was, because of the positive reaction from my sales team. They said the customers seemed to relax more without passing the paper back and forth! If you wish to try this, carefully print 0 through 9 along the bottom of a columned page. Also do the same with the alphabet. Then turn the page around and practice writing numbers and letters upside down until you get to be proficient. I got so I seldom ever had to turn the sheet around except for figuring some of the math. Although this gimmick served no true purpose, I can think back on the times this little icebreaker made me some good profits, and we all had fun with it.

WOULD YOU PLEASE NOT SPEAK!

Chisel this one in stone! When you have asked a closing question, the first one who speaks loses!

Think about it; although we cannot consider the customer's buying a new car as losing, he or she likely could have saved more money by staying silent.

When the buyer does break the pressure of that deafening silence, it is generally to ask some innocuous question that gives away the fact that they will agree, it was only to break the pressure to buy a little more time!

We answer the question and hold out our hand saying, "Congratulations!" Then shake the other person's hand immediately. Why, right then, and so quickly? Because in a high percentage of these situations, the husband had done all or most of the talking and his wife has consulted with him, and then with her full agreement, he has returned to negotiating.

Be careful here; because I've closed several thousand of these, and watched other sales associates *lose* many sales right at this moment. Remember the mental image; man consults with wife first, then makes the offer to you (watch the invisible marionette strings).

Now, he has asked you a question after your last offer to *relieve the pressure* while he thinks about it without those drums of decision beating; maybe he asks, "That car does have navigation, right?" You answer with, "Yes it does, and a good one!" Now without any more hesitance, you "assume the sale!" Hold out your hand and say, "Congratulations folks! I'll get it gassed up and cleaned for you," making eye contact with both while nodding your head, and turn promptly to the wife, hand out, big smile and say, "Thank you for your business, you'll love it!"

I have had hundreds upon hundreds of these exact scenarios over the years, and had I not gone from him directly and without another word in between, she would almost every time have another question or objection.

You'll read her mind when you see the look on her face before you thank her for the business. No, don't "congratulate" her, thank her! Why not? Because she will have a direct comeback, like, "Don't congratulate me; I didn't buy it; he did!" She will do so with anger in her voice and you will now have opened that proverbial "can of worms!"

You are now in for a variety of possibilities; from an angry, "We need to talk!" from her, to a meek and quiet, "Give us a few minutes" from him. Now you have single handedly reduced your 99 ½ percent sale to 50/50. That's how many of us learn!

Analyze now, if you had right off turned to the wife with a big, warm smile and said, "Thank you for your business! I'll get your car cleaned up and filled with gas."

You see how, one out of place word, can have a huge effect on your income. One word! Most people never learn this lesson throughout their entire career, because when these people blow out the door, the salesperson stupidly blames them for the inability to make a decision.

I know I am dwelling a lot on only one error, but if you think about how many couples you will work with in your career, the ones you *lose* could have paid for your house!

Rehash: Where this scenario went down the tubes was after shaking hands with him and saying "Congratulations!" which was perfect! You don't need to thank him because she is in charge, you turn immediately to her and you cannot congratulate her because it was her husband who had the audacity to shake your hand! A simple courtesy to her by asking, "Baby, can we buy it?" would have been perfect, but in all the excitement he forgot to ask the boss!

Now you need to save his ass! You do what he should have done; you thank her and let her know she's still in charge!

That's a lot of explaining, but use this same respect for all couples. Yes, gay people will have the same respect in their relationship, so get to know who is boss up front, and from that time on, every time the subordinate person speaks, a simple glance to the partner will be the courteous acknowledgement you need to sell a car!

Learn these few simple actions and you will sell so many more vehicles than your associates you won't believe it!

I cannot emphasize enough the importance of properly asking a closing question. Since we all know that after the question has been asked, the first one to talk loses, so we must make absolutely certain that the question has been properly asked!

NEVER TRY TO SELL COLOR TO A WOMAN

If your female customer says, "I don't like that color," why would you say anything? That was a statement, not a question, and it was also a test that doesn't require a response from you, so keep quiet; don't even nod in acknowledgement.

Maybe it's your last one of that particular model, and her mind may have deduced that it's the "last man standing" because of the color. So if it doesn't require an answer, it's not a question, so why bother?

You want the sale and it's the model she likes, so now what? Well first of all, why is it still here? Perhaps you should act surprised to see it? Maybe a remark like "It must have just come in; I didn't see it on the inventory list. Great! Let me run and get the keys so we can look at it."

She will most always go on a demo drive even if it isn't a color she likes. Now, just maybe on the test drive you may see someone eyeballing the car (it always happens) and a casual remark such as, "These (name the model) sure turn heads wherever they go!" Only *don't* say it's because of the color. Most likely, if you *never* bring it up again, she will buy it!

Some customers will ask, "Can't you check the other dealers to see if you can trade for a different color?" There are various responses you can make and they'd all better be "Yes, I'd be happy to." Then shut up, finish the test drive, and then, no matter what happens, if she likes the car, the color may not be a deal killer, and it's highly likely the subject never comes up again, because you passed the test.

Be smart enough to hope she will come around on her own to accept the color, but trying to *switch* a woman on color is like getting into a peeing contest with a skunk; you're gonna lose!

ASSISTANT BUYERS

Have you ever heard of a *maven*? I have worked in some of the largest cities in America, and in some societies it is common practice; such as in Jewish communities or other areas that you find English is a second language. Because the residents prefer to retain a closer tie to their homeland, they often will bring along a friend or advisor. In Yiddish, that person is called a maven.

The maven, or advisor, is most often someone the buyer respects. This person needs to be treated with that same respect, or even more so, by the auto salesperson.

All too often, the salesperson will be intolerant of this advisor and even downright rude and insulting! I have seen many incidents where managers would even get in the maven's face, telling them they are stupid and such! They usually always are forceful enough to win the argument, and when the customer up and leaves, the manager and salesperson can pat themselves on the back for not having to do any paperwork for a low commission, and their next move will be to have a soda or go smoke a cigarette to celebrate their stupidity!

You wouldn't think in these times we'd even have to discuss it, but there still remain many Neanderthals out there, and salespeople who learned their profession from this subspecies; so just a few words for any occasion a buyer brings a friend when shopping are in order.

Let's say a lady brings her girlfriend along, maybe more for security than advice. Treat the friend with respect, make sure they both have your business card, and include the friend in each conversation; as though she is also buying. The last thing you want do is insult or even slight the maven. You will lose every time.

Sometimes a second appointment may be necessary if the friend becomes argumentative, but you need to remain calm even though the third base coach ruins today's sale. It is highly likely in these circumstances that your buyer will also recognize how obnoxious her friend is being when she's showing off her knowledge, and the buyer will appreciate your courtesy to her friend.

Obnoxious or perhaps rude? Yes, but she has served her purpose and you have proven to the buyer that you are a courteous professional that she can trust. You *will* sell her on her next visit, and she will come alone!

Now if a man came in with another man who played the same obnoxious games, I'd most likely tell my people to, "Throw their asses out!" You see, there are sometimes limits to everyone's patience.

NO EVIL FROM THIS KNIEVEL

Now, since you have paid for it, and thanks for that, I will disclose what I feel has been the greatest money maker ever, and I got it from my good friend Nic Knievel! Yes, Evel's brother.

The following scenario is the method by which I have been more successful in closing sales than any other which I have ever used, and believe me, I've used them all. It was *gifted* to me by Nic very early in my career as an auto factory rep. I have further modified this to fit my own style, but this short question has earned for me, hundreds of thousands of dollars in commissions! Yes, these simple words.

It goes like this: Returning from the test drive, transitioning to the showroom, restrooms visited, refreshments offered, and now seated across from my buyers, paper in front of me, pen in hand, I smile and lean slightly forward, and making eye contact between the husband and wife, I ask, in my most sincere tone, "Dick, Jane, let me ask you this." I pause over a second, *"If I can make you happy with the numbers, will you buy this car and drive it home right now?"*

Await the answer and if you should draw a question, answer it, ask the same question again and sell a vehicle! Thanks Nic!

I have used this trial close ever since my first day on the retail side of selling cars. I started as a sales closer with a sales team of great people with a lot of experience, so I had to learn quickly! This very simple question, in these exact words, have never changed in over 18,000 sales and a smattering that got away!

PAYMENT BUYERS

It has often been said that "payment buyers" are the greatest gift to car people!

A payment buyer will typically try to keep his or her purchase price within the comfort zone based on a given monthly payment. As long as they can keep their purchase within a comfortable payment range they are happy.

The typical payment buyer hasn't changed a whole lot over the years, because everything they own, house, cars, furniture, and every purchase they make is based on how it affects their monthly budget.

Another indication that things haven't changed much is that we still make more money on payment buyers than any other type!

ANSWER QUESTIONS WITH QUESTIONS

The customer asks, "What's the least you'd take for it?" You respond with, "What's the most you'll pay?"

Customer, "Would you give me a trade allowance of $20,000?" You, "If I could, would you buy it right now?"

Customer, "What's your best price on this one?" You, "The most you'll pay and the least my boss will accept. Shall we drive it?"

TALK ABOUT VACATIONS

If you are selling in a dealership where a manager actually takes over negotiations after you create the initial offer to purchase, then when he or she is working with the Big Dog in the sales office, your job is to change the subject whenever the negotiator is absent.

Don't talk about the deal at all. Talk about their next vacation, trips to see family members, and paint pictures in their minds of them in their new car!

You now sell the fun, enjoyment and prestige they are about to welcome into their lives, but never talk about the numbers. You're selling only fun and stature in this particular situation.

THE RESTROOM IS A KEY

Picture this; you have been making good progress, but haven't yet been able to close your sale, one of your customers excuses themselves to use the restroom.

You've been negotiating hard and now your mind begins to wonder, "Should I have talked my boss into taking their last offer? I think they're going to leave," and worry starts to take hold; I say just relax, because when this person returns, almost always, they will walk right up and shake your hand! Normally, this is the man when he already received the silent "okay" from his wife.

He needed the bathroom break because he knows there will be a ton of paperwork to do, and he wants to get it done so he can get home before all his neighbors do, so they can notice his new car!

Naturally he has to leave it out for a while, while he cleans and rearranges his garage so his beautiful new "ride" will be happy. He may have to let the new car sit out for a day or two while he cleans a place for it; at least until his whole neighborhood has had a chance to admire it!

So when your buyer takes that pottybreak; don't panic. You just sold a car!

IF YOU WERE MY OWN BROTHER

Maybe you need a more emotional close, but I do not recommend that you use this very often. I don't even like it; but once in a while we meet a customer that is really fun to work with! After a bit of time, you find yourself really liking an individual and you feel close to this person. As I said, I don't like it because I detest phoniness, but if I get the right vibes, I can say it and mean it!

Depending on where you are your movement may vary, but let's say you're sitting at a table and you need a sincere closing statement with emotional quality. Reach forward, place your hand palm down on your customer's forearm, and in a calm, sincere voice, call him by name and say, "Bill; if you were my own brother, I'd tell you to buy the car." Then shut up! He will most likely buy. I'm sure there are occasions where the person still does not make the purchase, but it's very rare! Brothers are like that!

BACKING INTO A SALE

"Do you have to buy now?" Have you ever asked a customer that question? It works! Simply a thought to sometimes jar a customer back to reality when he's trying to be evasive.

Every so often, customers like to change their approach to keep us at bay. They make it very plain that today is only for looking, not buying!

Here's one that started sort of strange; as we were walking among the inventory, husband and wife speaking together loud enough for me to overhear. He's reminding her that he agrees when she labels him as an *impulse buyer*. I'm pretending to be busy reading stickers, when they speak to me, I pretend to be concentrating on something else and make them ask again.

He readily admitted to his wife while I *wasn't* listening, that when he gets in the mood for a new car, he wants the thrill of ownership right then, so now he is determined to do things differently this time around! This man knows that he is an *impulse buyer*, his wife agrees, but as I listen to parts of their conversation, I realize something they don't. She is also an impulse buyer without even realizing it! I know, because I can tell she's in charge, and he couldn't buy without her permission.

So as we look at different vehicles, they suddenly land on one that really excites them both. I remain casual, but professional and we go for a ride in it. After they both have driven it, I can tell it's like that adorable puppy in the pet shop, they're in love!

However, I had pretended to not have heard their previous agreement to *not* buy anything today, and now the only problem is to help them break that oath and go ahead and buy it!

So now I put on my best impression of either a salaried salesman, the owner's spoiled son, or just a salesman too stupid to come in out of the rain! I casually ask them, "Darth, Leia; you don't have to buy right now do you?" They both answer, "No" in surprise (a non-pushy salesman after their own hearts)! I answer, "That's good. Since this isn't something that you must do on the spot, let's go inside and see what the numbers look like on paper. That way, when you do decide, you'll know what the figures are. Okay?" I have offered to discuss numbers for them to think about; how very unusual and disarming! Car dealers just don't do that; this one does!

Picture us now as we walk to the showroom; no apprehension, totally relaxed, simply three friends discussing some numbers to think about for later on.

I will deviate slightly at this point from the approach I would use if we had already agreed to buy by tempering it slightly.

I now complete the appraisal slip, walk around their trade-in vehicle, notice scratches, dings and other value reducing flaws, while complimenting them on how well they've taken care of their vehicle. I will also mention how we are currently experiencing a shortage of clean, used cars, and if the current situation remains the same until they are ready to buy, the used car manager will probably pay a lot more than ever for their trade-in! That statement causes them to look into each other's eyes, which I always avoid noticing, and I can almost see dollar signs, hearts and candy kisses floating in the air above them! They both want a new car; *my new car*, and all they need is the justification I have given them without even asking!

You'll notice, I painted the picture and didn't attempt to ask them to even consider buying. In crude terms, I have set the hook, but I've left slack in the line; I'm not yet ready to reel in my new owner.

I'll now quickly finish gathering all the information I need, and I still have not asked them to buy. Why? Because if I did, I would defeating all of the built up excitement they will soon experience by making an impulse decision to surprise themselves with a new car; that feeling of total elation that will make them loyal to me for years to come!

Now, when I'm ready to keep my promise to "show them what the figures look like on paper," I can do so with two different people who are now excited to see what it would take to own it, but without any feeling of obligation or worries about making a decision; just three friends looking at numbers.

For the first time in their lives, these nice folks have a true friend in the car business, don't they? I have asked nothing of them, and I'm not even making them an offer. We are merely looking at an opportunity, but to get it, they'll have to *ask* their friend; me!

So now we read the proposal together as I had asked my manager to give my new friends a proposal so we may earn their business later on when they're ready. Now, they will mention at this point how they feel about the offer, but I am *not yet* their salesman, just their friend, so they tell me an honest figure that they would wish to have for their car *when they get ready* to buy a new one.

We now discuss, more as friends, and I say, "Darth, Leia; let me ask you this," and I do my long pause with a slight concentration wrinkle on my brow, "If you *did* decide to take the opportunity to make an offer right now," pause, "What number would have to be here (I point at the trade in spot) in order for you to buy the car and drive it home right now?" I smile and lean back slightly, they will come up with a number; and a quite reasonable one most always.

We learn early in life that the word "sign" is one that signals finality! We *never* use the term in the car business. All of our lives we think of *sign* as *costing* us something. "Signing our life away" etc.

In our business, we say, "Give me your *okay* on this and be sure to include your middle initial," or, "I'll need your okay here on the 'X' and please include your middle initial." Some people say, "Give me your John Hancock," and other similar words, but we are taught and then we teach others the same; to never use "sign!" Wrong; I will now!

I will on occasion break this ironclad rule when I really need to test my customer's willingness to put his or her word of honor up for mental collateral. I will, in cases like this, where I'm *backing* into a car deal.

I put the paper in front of them and I say, "Darth, Leia; sign here and make sure to include your middle initials." They never fail to ask while signing, "If your boss accepts, does that mean we're buying it?" I answer with, "Make sure you are serious about it, because if he says yes, you own it!"

I've never lost one when I've done it in this manner. As soon as I wrote the offer, the situation changed! I always joke and have fun with people, but backing into a sale like this, I am dead serious all the way through. One of the few times I am!

Incidentally, I taught all of my salespeople to get me involved whenever they needed help, so when it comes to working deals backwards, I generally worked it from scratch, because they received the commissions anyway; all I earned was my closing percentage.

BONUS TIME!

Learn this well; it works! So you have negotiated back and forth, and your manager has said, "Shake their hands." Now that you've done your dance of joy, you enter the showroom with a smile you could see for a mile!

Your buyers saw you the minute your foot came out of the door, and the look on your face, along with your walk of exuberance, tells them they just made a deal. They are excited! However, *before* you shake hands, you approach quickly, sit on the edge of your chair, lean forward and act out of breath, and as you make eye contact, you may look like James or Jane Bond passing secret information. You say, (and here the dollar figure changes to fit however gutsy you may feel), and you call them each by name, "Tim, Grace; *let me ask you this;*" and pause for effect, making direct eye contact, "Would you let $100 stand in your way?" Now don't move a muscle, try not to even breathe! Don't do anything but grab their hands and congratulate them when they accept!

If on the other hand, the people, generally the husband, suddenly stands up with some faked belligerence and makes a gesture to leave (he's bluffing), you laugh loudly and say, "Tim, don't get upset, you *bought* the car! I was just seeing if I was correct in my thinking. Congratulations!" Then you explain quickly that your boss and you were arguing, because he or she said you'd pay another $100 and you told him they wouldn't. Going on to say, "He bet me ten dollars on it, so thank you for making me a bonus!"

No, this is not all that complicated, you will never *lose* a customer by doing this bonus step, but on very few occasions you may have to react quickly to an objection, but you already know exactly how to react and what to say. Customers will never be upset with your asking for a mere $100 more. They knew by your previous negotiating that they were close to a deal; now they have won!

I've done this thousands of times and I can truthfully say, "I've never lost one!" It can get quite hairy at times though! Very few times has anyone ever objected, because I have prepared them for ownership and relaxed them by my smile and quick approach, and they are ready to shout for joy and start switching their personal belongings into their new car.

Now if you wonder if this is all worth it, let's take a look at the numbers. You may wish to vary the additional amount depending on what you feel is reasonable to achieve, but for now, let's look at where we're at.

For our example, let's take a salesperson who is paid 20% of the gross profit and sells an average of 15 cars a month. Since this $100 bonus works about 80% of the time, we can hope for 12 people who pay an additional $100 which amounts to $1,200 in profit, and at a 20% commission rate is $240 a month; $2,800 in additional commissions over a year's time; not a bad Christmas bonus!

Use your own personal numbers and percentages and you can see why this easily earned bonus is so worth going after. Play with these numbers, because even for all managers and salespeople, if they get nothing else from this book, this is the easiest "close" in the world. I had an entire career full of these $100 to $300 bonus bumps. If your negotiations stay friendly, this is super easy!

To analyze it a bit further, let's look at what we have created for this opportunity that we cannot afford to pass up! We have spent a lot of time with our buyer, we've walked inventories, we've test driven one or more vehicles, we've negotiated and now our customers can finally picture this beautiful vehicle in their yard! Is there any possible way that this picture could be shattered over a hundred or two dollars? Not a chance! Learn this well, and practice it to perfection.

Let me give you another example, because we all like money and think how much fun you'll have spending this free money.

$100 x 15 monthly sales = $1,500 x 80% success rate = 12 sales at $100 = $1,200 x 25% commission rate = $300 per month x 12 = $3,600 a year.

Now, if your dealership has managers (closers) who do the negotiating, they will also participate in this bonus at their percentage rate. When I first began doing this, my teams were ecstatic with the ease of earning these bonuses. Talk about building loyalty when you can think out of the normal procedure parameters without any danger of losing and earning extra money for your team and your dealership!

KEEP YOUR SEAT

So you're in heavy negotiation; the pressure has built (keep in mind that pressure builds diamonds), and your customer seems about to explode.

When you're good at your job, management will keep pushing you to new limits, so your job will likely never again be a "walk in the park!" Get used to it, because you'll be walking instead to the bank! Stay strong and learn to be fast on your feet.

Never apologize for your offer, but stand ready to *defend* it. Reemphasize that you have made a fair offer and never apologize for asking for "all the money!"

Quite often, when you have a certain breed of customer, he builds up pressure that must at some point require release. You can almost see this guy explode all over the place and you spending the rest of the day scraping "pieces of customer" off the walls! You know the type. More when, than if, your buyer suddenly jumps to his feet and you are sitting in front of an angry volcano. What do you do?

First of all, *never* stand up with him! If you did, now the picture would show two angry people in a boxing ring. You don't want to go there; this is *not* a confrontation. Your buyer needs this moment to let off steam, because he needs to make one more test to see if you'll suddenly and magically pull out a better offer from somewhere. Stay seated and calmly reassure him that you'd like to explain how your management arrived at those numbers.

Many salespeople react too quickly to such an explosion and they jump up with this Palooka, and now they are standing face to face. When this occurs, they likely will not have a chance to calm the customer down, because now he feels justified in his suspicion that you're trying to take advantage of him. That's what you telegraph when you stand up with him. Stay seated!

You then ask him to allow you to explain your proposal and he sits down. You will be amazed at how he has let off enough pressure that he will be a totally different person. Don't ever fear this kind of display. Many people need some kind of release for the pressure that the negotiating process creates while we are gradually building up profit!

They aren't mad at you per say, it's the "process" that they have to go through every time they buy a car. Show your consideration and empathize with him that you have to go through it too, and "I work here!" Now you laugh together and he respects you for not arguing and for being understanding.

Now all you have to do is explain that the numbers you presented to him were fair, but good for your dealership, "Now Jim, let's see if we can make the numbers a little more fair for you." All you do now is get your manager to make some sort of concession to your buyer and you need to prepare for a handshake. I promise you, he will buy from you every time!

I absolutely love working with this type of buyer, because they are open and honest. Most people get in his face and he blows out! I won't do that, because the angrier he is, the more money I'll make! While he's yelling and letting off steam, the cash register ringing in my ears is drowning him out!

Most salespeople at other stores have not let him release this pressure build up and he blew out without buying and he won't understand why, but he respects you!

This customer will very likely return to you for his next car, because you allowed him to be himself and express his feelings. This is one person who definitely needs to be regularly followed up on!

He will return to buy from you again, but only if you maintain contact *after* the delivery. If you don't he will lump you in with all the rest.

WHAT IF I ASKED YOU TO GUESS

Whenever you ask someone a question and you don't get the answer you need, here's what you do.

If I ask a customer a question and they answer with "I don't know" or "I don't remember," I follow up with, "If you had to guess?" That's when I get my answer!

People are reluctant to give an exact answer to a question the first time it's asked. For some reason, it may be that they don't wish to reply with the wrong answer, or to commit to what they feel is correct and turn out to be wrong. We can't demand a number and we can't say, "Think hard dummy!" So what do we do to get them to tell us what they know?

Easy; we allow them to get off the hook. We simply make certain that they understand the question, as, "Jesse, what's the amount you owe on your car?" He answers, "I don't have a clue." You ask, "If you had to guess?" Jesse immediately responds with, "Ten thousand nine hundred fifty-four dollars." He is only *guessing* of course!

Try this with your friends, it works amazingly well! You can have a lot of fun, and this simple statement will make you a lot of money as well!

THE $1400 SANDWICH

Ever had a $1400 sandwich? One of my salespeople did. He said I could tell you in case you were curious about how it was. This happened a while back, but it bears talking about.

This happened while I was running a sales team in an upper-end dealership. We had our salespeople on a rotating "up system" so they weren't loitering around the showroom. Our rather sophisticated clientele were thus protected from gazing on our "wretched staff" (just joking); but let's just say it was a classy joint, with only one prominent desk in the corner of the showroom.

I was in my usual place, enjoying one of the 60 cigarettes I would smoke that day, and my salesman who was *up* was outside with me. Let's call him "Ray." Because that was his name and he wanted me to use it so the incident would remind him forever of that day!

Ray had been partying hard the night before, and let's just say, he was not happy about being on the early shift. In fact, I had to tell him to be quiet and suffer; I did not appreciate my people coming to work in a state of disrepair.

He kept asking me if he could go to lunch early and I kept reminding him that he was on a list of eight people and if he gave up his place, he went to the bottom of the rotation. It had been rather slow for traffic the last couple of days, and we hadn't even had one customer so far at 11:00 when I finally succumbed to his grousing and begging and let him go to lunch.

Ray walked across the street to the restaurant and not even a minute after he walked in their door a car pulled in and parked right up in front of the showroom. My salesperson who was next in line walked out to greet the couple, and the husband pointed at a vehicle on the lot that was the center of our outdoor display.

He emphatically stated as he pointed, "We're buying that one!" A half hour later Ray ambled sheepishly back to the lot, walked up to me and asked, "How much did my BLT cost me?" I said, "Fourteen hundred dollars!" Neither Ray nor I will ever forget that one! Ray was a big help in the next few sales meetings! I felt sorry for Ray, because he took a lot of ribbing to his already bruised ego.

SMILE AT THE PRICE

If "the feel of the wheel is half the deal" as we like to say, what's the other half? That's the part where the time invested in the demo drives comes to fruition in the actual negotiations and sale!

We all seem to have cutesy and subtle ways to ask people to buy, and the absolute best time to do so is right after the test drive! If you have a man and woman together, they must both have been given the opportunity to drive it; an absolute must!

You have earned the right to ask the customers to buy, but you must ask them, because it is not usually the case where they jump out and say, "Let's go in and do the paperwork, we want to buy it!" I wish it were so, but asking someone to buy is a moment where everything a salesperson has done so far is in *earning* the right to ask the *heaviest* question ever!

There are many variances of how one goes about asking someone to buy, and most salespeople have a real problem at the point where the question should be asked. The customer is expecting you to ask them to buy it, and if you don't, then they would be thinking that maybe in your mind, you don't think it's the right vehicle for them. After all, the last time they were at a dealership, the salesman asked them as soon as they picked the car they wanted to see! So you had now better get to the point rather quickly, you've *earned the right*!

Now you have options in how to ask. One way I like is, "Hank, Sally; if I can make you smile at the price, would you buy this car and drive it home right now?" Now, you shut up and wait! Yes, no matter how long they take. You can ask people to buy, but always remember that, no matter how long it takes, you *must* wait for them to answer! For this reason, you'd better hope they were listening and that they understood.

Sometimes to lessen the building pressure, they will be compelled to ask you a question. If they do, answer the question and repeat your closing question, "So, Sally, Hank; can we go ahead and take it home right now?"

The most important part of this is the "right now." Not today, tonight or anything other than *right now*! I have seen far too many times where after several hours of negotiating where a customer suddenly stands up and thanks the salesperson for their time and says, "Thanks for your time, we'll think about it and get back to you later."

I have also watched salespeople and managers arguing with the customer about the fact that they said they would buy it, and most always it got so heated, that by the time it ended, they would never return! This never happened to my salespeople, because they handled the write-up (offer) differently and a lot more professionally! No, not bragging, but they all knew and practiced over and over.

I actually have watched a sales manager get in a customer's face while pushing the write-up sheet in front of the husband and yelling, "You signed this and it says you would buy the car and drive it home today." While the manager was frothing at the mouth, the customer took the paper away from his face and said, "I signed this saying I would buy it *today*, and there's a lot of *today* remaining" and stuck it back in front of the manager saying, "See!" I won't repeat what he called him, but the words initials were A.H.; then when the manager had looked at the agreement again, the customer grabbed back the sheet and said, "However, for us the day is all done and so are we!" With that, he tore his and his wife's signatures off the bottom and they stormed out leaving the papers on the floor!

At least their keys were still on the desk (just kidding). That brings up another point of contention that I may as well address in the next chapter.

TRADE-IN KEYS

In most dealerships when a customer is trading in a vehicle, the salesperson takes the keys, along with the offer to purchase (write-up) to the sales office for an appraisal. It is common practice for management to retain the keys until the customer eventually "buys or flies."

Many times you will hear people ask, "Where are my keys, do you have my keys?" It has always been common for the majority of dealers to hang on to the keys, because it's kind of a *glue* to keep the customer captive until they've tried every possible way to make the sale.

I've seen some pretty rough operations, and met customers who at times in the past had experienced having a manager literally toss their car keys, including the rest of their keys in many cases, on the dealership's roof! Our car business today is a far cry from its very crooked past!

I'm glad I came along after the brutality, but I've met so many victims of abuse in cities where the old diehard Neanderthals were still hanging on when they should have been hanging from trees!

Anyway, my favorite approach to the key situation is to return from my appraisal (when I'm the used car manager) and walk up to the customer and lay the keys on the desk by them. Don't hand them back, simply lay them there. As simple as it sounds, those keys act as a bond of trust to keep the customer from leaving. This simple courtesy is a gesture of trust, and the majority of customers will *never* reach for them. It would be an indication that they don't trust you.

If for some reason they do pick up their keys and put them in purse or pocket, it doesn't mean you should panic. All you need worry about is staying professional. Besides, the used car manager hid their car in the shop (just joking)!

BAD WORD; WASH YOUR MOUTH OUT!

It is amazing how so many supposed professional salespeople can make such innocuous and stupid comments!

Like walking up to an elderly customer and asking, "How are you young lady?" or "How are you young man?" If you are that stupid, please kick yourself right in the ass and then go resign! You may as well have asked, "How are you dumb old farts doing today?"

To me, I've heard and had personal *sit downs* with those people a lot, because if one is so absolutely stupid as to make such an ignorant comment, then there must be some more "stupid" lingering in their heads and they couldn't sell water to Smokey the Bear! I don't wish to belabor the point, but this ignorance is all over the place, and in all businesses, but our people are paid too well for customers to tolerate that amount of stupid from them.

Oh yes; what about the older salesperson who comes up with the "How are you, young man or young lady?" This shows a stupid lack of respect that costs everyone money. Change them or fire them!

We need to select carefully before we ask questions, as a customer will normally answer about three of them before losing patience with us. They came to look and not jump through hoops for the privilege.

I hope you don't do the, "Are you buying today or just kicking tires?" Or, "Is that the car you're trading in to us today?" Cute, but shallow and unprofessional!

Ask questions like, "Is this the car you're replacing?" Replacing is polite; trading is implying deal!

When you're trying to qualify whether a person is a buyer or not, remember this basic qualifier; there are only three reasons for a person to enter our showroom; to use the phone, to visit the restroom or to buy a car! So if they are not on the phone and not sitting in the bathroom, sell them a car!

THE OTHER TYPE OF TIP

This one is called a gratuity. In car talk, it translates to, "Thank you for the customer and please send me more!"

I know a lot of salespeople who hand out hundreds of dollars in cash every single year to people who have referred buyers to them. Even if you are referred a buyer from someone you work with. I guess maybe I should say; *especially* from one you work with!

I am reticent about this, but in our business we often ignore policies, such as those that forbid the receptionist from receiving gratuities for referrals to individual salespeople. Oftentimes management won't be so critical or quick to condemn an aggressive salesperson if this referral is from that person's friend, and not from a regular sales call.

Every person who has something to do with making you money should receive some form of compensation. It's called, "investing in your future!"

STEALING THE TRADE-IN

Figuratively, not literally! If you're selling in a dealership that usually offers the actual cash value (ACV) for the trade-ins (there are fewer of these than ever), ask them to give you some more room.

By that I mean, as you become better at selling and *holding on* to customers when they object to the figures, you may occasionally request the manager to "hit you hard on the trade!" This should be a lot lower than ACV, to allow you a chance to earn a higher profit!

An example would be if you have the feeling that your customer really hates his trade, or if he's bragged about buying his current car from an uncle that practically gave it to him, this is an opportunity for you to think outside that normal procedure you are so accustomed to.

Do you not think that your management would pay you a commission on every dollar of profit you earn? Then what is wrong in both of these examples with tipping off management to the fact that the customers may just accept a lot less on their trades? Maybe two or three thousand dollars less! If this happens and you earn $3,000 more profit on the sale, do you think that's bad? The salesperson is like a periscope on a submarine. Only you have a true picture of the customer, and if you think you can make more money, tell the boss to *go for it!*

Buyers often forget we're listening because we're on their side if we play "good guy – bad guy" as some dealerships still do. I've heard customers brag about the fender-bender they were in where the other driver's insurance company not only repaired their car, but paid them thousands of dollars for the *diminished value* side of it. Maybe even to the tune that they're debating upon trading it in or giving it to their grandchild!

Let's say the car is worth $6,000, but they've got full value for it as far as they're concerned and to them it holds no real value. Sell hard on that one; that you need cars like theirs for those buyers that need basic transportation, and you always need reliable used cars. Never let it happen where you can keep a *moneymaker trade* in the equation to remove it from the transaction.

Now if you get them to accept $1,000 for instance, and your used car manager stocks it in for $4,000, you just picked up an additional $3,000 on which you will be paid. If you were working on a $3,000 gross profit, you now will be paid on $6,000 gross profit!

Anytime you can influence a transaction like this, you are paid directly for your efforts! Every single dollar you can save on what your manager has to allow for the trade-in goes into profit in which you participate!

I have earned so many thousands of dollars by doing this; I couldn't begin to add it up!

On the other side of the equation, never – ever *steal* from your dealership! Allow me to explain this very innocent, but common theft: The salesperson is badly in need of another sale and any sale will work; maybe to hit a bonus or one more for the next paycheck. So to *hedge their bet*, they con the manager into taking a lesser profit deal out of their personal fear of further negotiating efforts. Stay strong!

DOING SOMETHING FOR ITS EFFECT ON OTHERS

Before I entered the retail end of the car business, I was the automobile manufacturer's liaison. I was attending a sales meeting at one of our dealer's operations at which my good friend Nic Knievel was manager.

Nic knows I tell this story. Anyway, Nic mentioned to me before the meeting that his salespeople were letting their hair grow too long, sprouting beards and so forth. So he said, "Watch my cure for it!"

There we were; Nic on stage, and about 40 salespeople and managers in the room. Nic was teaching how he wanted a certain task performed when he stopped in mid-sentence and just stared at the bleachers. A minute went by without any noise, not even a cough, when suddenly in a loud voice he said, "Hank, I told you to get a haircut! That's the last time; go downstairs and pick up your check, you're all through!" Then after the poor guy sheepishly left the room, Nic calmly finished the meeting, handed out bonuses and awards and we were done.

Then Nic and I went to our favorite restaurant to discuss business. Returning three hours later, I couldn't believe my eyes; every person in the sales department had somehow managed to get haircuts! They were all neatly shaven, no beards, very few moustaches and shined shoes. They were the most professional looking sales force of any of my dealers!

Nic said he had allowed his people to get sloppy, but just one example (sacrificing his weakest salesperson) allowed for the change; and at first I thought, how callous! Then I understood when he explained that he didn't really care to or even *dare* to treat his managers or his best salespeople that harshly or they may quit on him. Therefore, he used his worst salesperson as an example and what a change! When the dealer returned from lunch, he shook Nic's hand and remarked on how professional everyone looked. A sales force can easily go downhill in appearance over time, so one must strive to look professional!

Nic further explained to me that because the job he had required so much effort, that his team of managers had followed him through several moves, and he would never take the chance of breaking up his loyal and professional team. That's why he never dressed them down; in private or in front of anyone else. As tough as he was, I appreciated that he valued talent.

I use this example for everyone who has personnel issues to contend with, because I have used similar methods to improve dealerships after learning the subtle tricks.

Rest in peace Nic! Thanks.

THE COLUMBO CLOSE

I have always picked interesting and effective methods of body language from every source available. Early in my closing career, Peter Falk starred in the TV detective series *Columbo*. After the first few episodes, I had developed what I called the *Columbo Close*, and it has made me *huge* amounts of money! Columbo always had a semi-stumbling method of investigating crimes, where he would be leaving a room, and suddenly turn, as if deep in thought, and say, "Just one more question." I liked it so much that I immediately adopted the technique and tailored it for the car business.

When closing a sale, the pressure must be eased from time to time. Whenever I make the next pass, I try to get all of the *movement* I can. I'll present the numbers given me by the sales manager (or myself, if I'm doing it all), and I know that I must get all the movement (willingness to pay more and take less for his or her trade-in) from the buyer that I can. It is important that both sides continue to give, and end up compromising with a mutually acceptable agreement. If the customer just moves a *little* toward my offer, then I must move *a lot*. Working a deal means structuring the plan whereby we can make a sale by meeting in the middle. Now if the customer is fighting the process, and wants to rush it, I'll do it in stages, and here's where the Columbo Close comes into play. I'll write down what they just offered and start to walk away to go back to my manager, then suddenly I pause, turn and either lean on the table (if there's room without invading the customer's space) or I'll oftentimes just stand there, or even just squat down alongside, *without* sitting, and say something like, "Now, just in case the boss says he wants blah, blah, what should I hit him with?" Customers see this is a sincere concern that I feel their offer will be turned down, and "I want to do right by them." They will give some answer which is usually an indication that they may be willing to go higher but, "See what he says." Now when they answer; I sit back down, but just on the *front* edge of the chair, like I'm planning to depart quickly. In actuality, I now will push for a higher offer from them! My purpose is to make as few passes as I can, as if we run back and forth too many times the customer will perceive this as us grinding on them, and eventually we'll wear out our welcome and lose.

Columbo enables a person to cut the negotiations in half if done properly. I can make a pass, get a bump, use Columbo, sit back down and get another bump! My salespeople immediately noticed my new technique, because it was a natural for selling situations. Whenever there has been a tense or confrontational situation with a customer, I immediately diffuse the situation by taking what they offer, depart, and show them it's going *their way;* and then using Columbo, I'm back in the driver's seat! Remember, your customers will always pay more for a great performance! They want a show; give 'em one!

I realize that I have dwelled on the Columbo Close for a long time, but the art of negotiating is so important that it needs to be perfected, and one cannot prepare too much! Practice this technique with a close friend or your spouse, and they can help critique your performance.

Especially important in keeping a long negotiation from getting tense, is to not drag out the *grinding*. You know you need a big bump, and yet your customer has reacted negatively, and given you just a token increase and has gotten tense; you now diffuse the tension, and use Columbo to reopen your request, and not totally sitting back down, keeps them from getting tense again. This casual body language takes the pressure off, and will still get you some movement! Just the mere fact that you are squatting down alongside the table or desk, instead of sitting back down, keeps the situation from getting tense and you impart a genuinely professional image.

You can see the incredible difference that *body language* makes in negotiating sales. My *Columbo* method makes the difference in your being good at your job or being great!

GLOSSARY OF TERMS

Car talk from our early days that has followed us to the present.

3 on the tree — Old 3-speed column shift.

4 on the floor — Standard 4-speed.

5,6 — Slang used by loan company as a code to remind the loan officer to use furniture (**Sticks**) for collateral on down payment loan. Like the kids' counting chant; 5, 6, pick up sticks. "Pick up sticks" on a UCC collateral form, so if the loan defaults, you have collateral value.

Advance the clock — This used to happen a lot in Northern states when Canadian residents came to the United States to buy cars. The tariff was much lower on vehicles going into Canada with 750 or more miles, so dealers put the cars on the hoist in drive with the engine running, and waited for the desired mileage to hit; then the Canadian customer drove it home, and the fees were so much less, as to Canada, it was a "used" car.

ACV — Actual cash value – what the vehicle goes in the books for. Wholesale; *not* what *book* value says.

A.G. — Attorney General. This is a subject we hope never to talk about.

App — Credit application.

Available sales manager (page) — When this page goes out, the *desk* needs a closer to go in on a deal, and if it's not a page for the salesperson's closer by name, it probably means to send a closer behind another closer who's having trouble. It's like yelling "hey Rube" at a circus.

Back end profit — The profit created by the finance manager (**business manager**); sources include finance, insurance, extended warranties, etc.

Back of book — Generally a reference to a vehicle that has a value less than the used car guide's "suggested wholesale value." Also a reference to a slovenly or unkempt person. Consider "book" as "even."

BDC — Business development center (phone room).

Beater — Auction piece – not worth taking in trade.

Bird-dog — Someone who sends in a customer and generally receives a reward.

Book – book out — Book is what the used car guide in the area says the wholesale and retail values are. I.e. wholesale book may be $20,000, but the true value (**ACV**) may be $16,000.

Bubble — Used when we let a customer leave with an idea that he will get a deal much better than we actually can do. When he returns, we have to "burst his bubble" and get him to accept reality.

Bullpen — Where fresh trades are placed to await for clearance of funds, contracts and titles.

Bump — An increase in payment or price.

Buried in the trade— A customer who owes much more on his trade-in than it's worth. If they're far out of line, we say, "They have to 'dig up' just to be buried."

Business manager — Title used to professionalize and disguise the finance manager. Finance is a word not allowed in the sales transaction. Instead we use "carry a balance" or similar words whenever possible.

Butternose the trade — Leave the trade-in out of the picture because the customer owes too much to get out of it; with the idea of letting it go back to the bank as a repossession. This was done a lot, years ago.

Buy rate — The interest rate the bank charges the dealership. The dealer may then increase this rate to the customer and receive the difference as profit. Normally the dealer may raise this rate up to three percent or more over the buy rate; if the customer holds still for it. The dealer keeps the extra profit.

Cherry — Perfect car – hardly broken in.

Cherry picker — Salesperson who sits back and waits for "select" ups and only takes one when it looks ideal; such as the elderly couple in a several year-old car.

Chisler — A customer who negotiates beyond reason for every last dollar.

Chute — Another term for the auto auction. Cars *coming through the chute*.

Clock — Odometer reading.

Close — To negotiate a deal until the customer buys it. The deal is done (closed).

Closer — The assistant manager or sales manager who negotiates for the "house."

C-note — One hundred dollars.

Co-jock — Cosigner or co-maker.

Credit bandit — Customer with bad credit.

Curbing — Salesperson is selling his personal vehicle to a dealer's customer.

Dealer trade — Where dealers swap new, untitled vehicles to assist one another. Each dealer pays the other's exact invoice amount.

Demo — Demonstrator or demonstration. A "**demo**" drive, or if a manager is supplied a company car as a perc, he or she has a "**demo**."

Desk — Person in charge of the deal (sales manager).

Downer — Same as **sewered**.

Downstroke — Amount of cash available for the down payment.

Eyeball — A vehicle with a beautiful appearance – a showpiece. The car has "eyeball."

F & I — Finance and insurance.

F & I guy or gal — Manager who handles finance and insurance and finalizes the transaction.

Finance reserve — Potential profit made by raising the interest rate the customer will pay over the dealer's "**buy rate**." This difference is paid to the dealer in stages, as the finance interest is earned while the rest is held in reserve by the bank in case the contract becomes prepaid, in which case the dealer's participation ends.

Flake — Someone with bad credit.

Fleet (sarcastic) — *Full List (price) Each and Every Time.*

Fleet department — Generally people who work with business accounts; or *anyone they can get.*

Flip — Another word for **turn** or turn-over to another salesperson.

Float — When a dealer sells a vehicle and gets paid for it by cash or on a finance contract, but does not pay it off at the bank that handles his flooring "**floorplan**." This is a dangerous practice and generally indicates a big problem at that dealership.

Floor check — Inventory checks of a dealer's "**floorplan**" done by the bank at random to make certain that any unaccounted for vehicles are paid off to keep a dealer "in trust." If a dealer has sold vehicles that he has not paid for, he is "**floating**" and may likely be immediately shut down. I have had to do that when I worked for banks.

Floorplan — New and used vehicles that are available for sale on a dealer's lot and that his bank advances the money for him to operate with. The bank holds the titles and MSOs (manufacturers statement of origin) for collateral. Most dealers need this line of credit in order to stock enough product to keep them in business.

Floor whore — A salesperson who spends all their time "grabbing ups" and who never follows up or prospects for business.

Fluff & buff — Detail of a vehicle. Clean and wax.

Foursquare — Basic structure of initial offer. The old process by which a blank sheet of paper is divided into four squares.

FNG — F*#king new guy.

A **Franklin** — A $100 dollar bill.

Front end profit — The profit made on the selling of the vehicle and added accessories sold by the sales department.

Geesel — One thousand dollars.

Get-ready — Place where sold vehicles are cleaned and "prepped" for delivery.

Going for the throat — After a trial close (see **testing the water**); if the buyer seems receptive, then like a wolf, we tear out the jugular.

Got the blinders on — Customer's excitement where they can only see the good parts; like blinders on the sides of their eyes.

A **Grant** — A $50 dollar bill.

Grape — Person who is easy to "pick their pocket." Also called a **lay down** or **mullet**.

Gray market car — Brought in to the United States outside of regular importing channels, i.e. factory, to avoid tax and tariffs. These are difficult to license. This happened primarily with Mercedes and other expensive imports years ago.

Grinder — Standard transmission; "stick shift."

Gross — The gross profit on which you receive a commission.

Guts — Vehicle's interior. Interior fabric choice; leather or cloth.

Gypsy — An ethnic group or wholesaler, generally from Romania. Entire families (tribes) work in teams; all in the wholesale and retail car business. Almost a generic term.

Hammer the check — When the salesperson is sent to the customer's bank to get cash for the down payment check. Done mostly when the manager feels the customer may "**come out of the ether**," and when he does he may stop payment on the amount to try and negotiate further or trade back (unwind).

Heat & ice — Heater; from the days where manufacturers built cars for the Southern states without heaters and for the Northern states without air conditioning to keep costs down.

Hit — A trial close.

Hit figure — The starting offer on the trade allowance (low).

Hold check — The customer writes a check that the dealer holds for an advance date for deposit when the funds will be covered.

Holdback — An amount added into a dealer's invoice to indicate a higher "cost." This **holdback** is then automatically deposited into the dealer's account (by the manufacturer) the minute an **RDR** (retail delivery report) is entered in the computer, indicating a retail sale.

A Hole in the roof — Moon roof or sunroof.

Home run — Huge profit – all there was.

Hunskee — One hundred dollars.

Ice — Air conditioning.

Ink — get the ink — Signed contract.

Invoice — The amount a dealer pays the manufacturer for the vehicle, but not necessarily the true cost. Dealer incentives plus holdback will still come back to the dealer.

Jack (Jack-off) — Someone wasting your time.

Jonesin' — High on drugs or adrenalin.

Keeper — In reference to a trade-in that the used car manager will keep on the lot for retail sale.

Kick the trade — Try to work a deal without the trade-in, because he either wants too much or he's buried. Note: Convince him to buy now and sell the trade himself.

Kiss the paper — Dealer guaranteeing the finance contract to the bank. If the customer defaults, the dealer pays off the bank.

Knock — A decrease in value, payment or price.

Lay down — One who "flops over" on the first "**pencil**" and buys whatever we present to him.

Lessee — Person who leases.

Lessor — Lease company.

Liner — Salesperson who is "on the line" (selling). Generally in stores that employ closers.

Loaded — A vehicle with most all equipment/options.

Lookie-Loo — Someone who always seems to "be looking" and can't decide.

Lot attendant (porter) — All-around "gopher" to shuttle vehicles; basically used by the sales manager to do all the "grunt" jobs around the sales department; wash cars for delivery, run errands, pick up lunch, etc.

Lot lizard — Lot attendant. Referred to as a "porter" in many stores.

Maven — Yiddish term to describe their custom of bringing along an advisor for negotiating and moral support (third base coach).

Mooch — A detestable individual who keeps negotiating for trivial amounts.

Mouse House — The old term for the finance company who made "down payment" loans to buyers. The words "mouse 'em" meant to procure the money in down payment required by the bank by having the customer "secretly" borrow it. Collateral for the loan was often their furniture and belongings (**sticks**). Also called the **trap**, as in mousetrap.

Mr. Brown (page) — Pages like this were often a signal to the sales staff that a call was coming in on a special number. This was a number only used for ads such as; "Call Mr. Brown for a free credit check." Customers calling for **Mr. Brown** would be answered only by certain people who specialized in credit challenged customers.

Mr. and Mrs. Gross — A couple driving in who look like they will be easy and solid buyers, and who will produce a large gross profit.

M.S.O. – Manufacturers statement of origin — The vehicle's "birth certificate."

Mullet — A low on the food chain buyer – bad credit.

Music — Stereo systems; was optional in earlier years.

Net-net — The dealer's true cost of a vehicle; invoice minus "**holdback**," minus factory incentives.

Nickel — Five hundred dollars.

Note — Seldom used anymore, but was a promissory note used when a check was not available, and redemption by the customer had to be made before payments began. Also references a check.

Odo — Odometer reading.

One legger — Person whose spouse is not there, but will be involved in the buying decision. One leggers are given only enough information to excite them enough to bring in their spouse.

Open floor — Situation where salespeople are free to come in to work when they are off shift. Those scheduled need to be there, but the sales are "open" to other salespeople as well.

Pack — An amount added to the invoice or cost of a vehicle on which the dealer will not pay a commission. Example: If a vehicle cost is $20,000.00 and there is a pack of $600.00, it means that the salesperson will be paid on any earnings over $20,600.00. There is zero commission paid on the first $600.00 of profit.

Qualify — To ask enough questions to determine a customer's needs and wants, and to ascertain what it will take to sell them a vehicle.

Pencil — The offer from the "desk" to the buyer in writing.

Pickie — A "pickup payment" to be made before the regular payments begin; generally secured by a "**hold check**" and used for additional down payment to meet the lender's requirement, and where the buyer is short of funds at the time of purchase.

Pink slip — The title to the vehicle. The term often used by managers in other states, but originated in California, as that was the color of their titles. Managers in other states adopted it to "sound cool." As in, "get the pink."

Plain Jane — Stripped car – see Sally Rand.

Potlot — Used car lot with cheap "**beater**" cars.

Pounder — Big **swat**, a large profit. Better than average gross profit.

Pulling my chain — See Jack.

Queege — Small dollar amount.

Rattle can — A spray can with either paint or clear lacquer to improve the appearance of a car or cover up mistakes, flaws and damage. Used a lot on engines and tires to make them look new.

RDR — Retail delivery report. Note: Sent by computer to the manufacturer. Triggers the warranty (new only).

Reader — A check or promissory note.

Recourse — Done when the dealer has so much potential profit in a sale that he guarantees the bank the customer will make the payments, or the dealer will pay off the contract after the bank repossess the vehicle and returns it to the dealer. **Recourse** can be partial (certain number of payments) or full; the entire length of the contract. This was used mainly by the "fast track" operators where the bank would fund anything the dealer wrote. Such high volume operations didn't have time to discuss each contract; they "**rolled**" anything; also called "**kissing the paper.**" This method did not require the bank's credit approval.

Red guts — Red interior.

Reg (registration) — A document to show where the vehicle is licensed and titled. Includes address, county and state.

Ring — Auto auction.

Roach — Bad car.

Roll — Delivery of a vehicle.

Rolled around by a two-bitter — Shopped to other dealers for higher bid by a wholesaler.

Roof — Sunroof or moon roof.

Rotation — Term for method of taking **ups**. Rotation means taking customers in turn, and rotating to the back of the sales line.

Rubber — Tires.

Sally Rand — A basic auto – no extras, no add-ons. Note: Sally Rand was an early burlesque dancer and actress who had been accused of dancing nude; thus the other term, **stripper**.

Scratch a reader — Write a check.

Sewered — Down in the dumps. Bad attitude.

Sheep — Customer who is all too willing to follow to the slaughter.

Shop — Service department.

Shut — Slang to **close**, or complete the sale.

Shutter — Closer. I once had license plates that said; SHUTTR. Everybody thought I was a photographer.

Skate — **Skater** — A salesperson who jumps in front of another salesperson.

Sled — A car of marginal value.

Slider — Power moon or sun roof.

Snakes — Anything that is not completely understood or properly explained that could go wrong if discovered by the customer.

S.O.T. or **sold out of trust** — Where a dealer has sold a vehicle and HAS not paid it off on his **floorplan**. This is also called "running a float" and is a serious problem that will cause a bank to shut down the operation.

Special finance — A separate department in the dealership whose people only deal with credit challenged customers. They specialize and become an indispensable asset to a dealer whose regular finance managers don't want to endure the enormous work necessary to babysit these lengthy transactions.

Spin the clock — Roll back the odometer to decrease the indicated mileage (illegal today, but not earlier).

Straight sell — Where the salesperson works the entire transaction with instructions from the manager. If additional help to close the sale is required, the manager goes out as a courtesy.

Sticks — Furniture – sometimes used for collateral when customer obtains financing for their down payment.

Still in the crate — The old "woody" station wagon.

Straw purchase — Person buying and financing a vehicle under their name for someone else; mostly because of the actual recipient's credit being bad. This is without the lender's knowledge.

Stripper — Stripped model – no extra equipment.

Strokes — Monthly payments (make the strokes).

Switch — Where it is necessary to lead or force the customer to select a vehicle different from the one he initially wanted to purchase. Mostly done to make more profit.

System — We all have a system, but in the car business it refers to the liner-closer (system house) operations.

Swat — Same as **pounder**. Big gross profit.

Tags — Current registration and expiration.

Taillights — The old saying is that "the deal is never done until you see taillights." The last thing you see as the customer drives over the curb.

Technician — Auto mechanic.

Testing the water — Attempting a huge profit offer, but doing so lightly to "take the buyer's temperature." It's like sticking only your big toe in the bathtub.

T.O. — **Turn** or turn over, as in hand off the customer to another salesperson or **T.O.** to the manager.

Trade — Car being traded in.

Trade allowance — The figure shown as the amount deducted for the trade-in from the agreed upon purchase price.

Trap — Finance Company (see **Mouse House**).

Trial close — See **testing the water**.

Tunes — Radio.

Turd — See "Beater."

Turn — To "turn over" the customer to another salesperson or manager.

Two-bitter — Old term for a wholesaler from years back who would pick up a car from one lot and go to other dealers to see if he could sell it for at least two bits (twenty five dollars) profit and hopefully a lot more.

Under the ether — Customer is excited about purchasing the new vehicle; like having the anesthesiologist applying the "feel good" medicine.

Up — Customer – (up to bat).

Up money — In reference to a vehicle that is calculated to bring a value greater than the wholesale "book" value.

Upside-down — When a customer owes more on his trade than its' actual cash value (**ACV**).

Write-up — Offer.

W.T. (wretched turd) — An ugly or bad vehicle.

ABOUT THE AUTHOR

Gary Swanson is living in Southern Utah. Several years as a real estate broker didn't hold the same excitement for him as the car business, so he now spends his time with his wife and two schnauzers hiking and exploring.